❖ (Above) Interior
of present studio
with JANUARY
STUDY I in the
background. 1987.
Photograph by
Nancy Crow.

# NANCY CROW
## QUILTS AND INFLUENCES

"written to help understand"

❖ *(Right) March sky photographed by Nancy Crow in 1982.*

❖ *(Left) March sky, 1982, photographed by Nancy Crow.*

The sky became an influential presence after we moved to our farm in 1979. I never noticed it when living in town. With flat fields and few buildings obscuring the horizon, the sky loomed large, and I began photographing it often at night handholding my old NIKON FM at terribly slow settings. I was fascinated by the color patterns, but I was also training my eye to see in a new way.

❖ *(Next page) MARCH SKY (in progress), 1982. This quilt grew out of my need to translate some of the "spirit" and the "energy" of the sky as seen in these two photographs. Photograph by Nancy Crow.*

# NANCY CROW
## QUILTS AND INFLUENCES

*Text by Nancy Crow*
*Foreword by Jean Robertson*

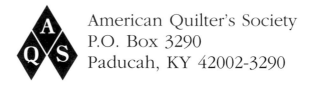

American Quilter's Society
P.O. Box 3290
Paducah, KY 42002-3290

Published by the
American Quilter's Society,
P.O. Box 3290, Paducah, KY 42002-3290

Printed and Bound in Hong Kong by Everbest
through Four Colour Imports, Ltd.

Material selection and book design by Nancy Crow.
Kay Blackburn Smith, production coordinator for AQS.

**Library of Congress
Cataloging in Publication Data**

Crow, Nancy, 1943-
NANCY CROW: Quilts and Influences/text by Nancy Crow;
foreword by Jean Robertson.
p. cm.
ISBN 0-89145-944-8: $29.95
1. Crow, Nancy, 1943- –Sources. 2. Crow, Nancy, 1943- –Family.
3. Quilts–United States–Themes, motives.
4. Textile fabrics–United States–Themes, motives.
I. Title.
NK9198.C76A4 1989    746.9'7'092–dc20  89-83587 CIP
First Edition

❖ *(Preceding photograph) Nancy Crow in her studio in front of MEXICAN WHEELS I, 1988. Photograph by Kevin Fitzsimons.*

❖ *(Opposite page) Carol Bobo, Nancy Crow, Jean Alexander Greenwald in front of mask collection in kitchen of Nancy Crow, 1988. Photograph by Nathaniel Stitzlein.*

# THE PHOTOGRAPHERS

### Carol Bobo

Carol and Jean traveled with me up to Loudonville, Ohio, my hometown, to photograph the antique quilts brought into the Cleo Redd Fisher Museum by residents of my home county, Ashland County.

### Nancy Crow

I took the photographs of all the quilts no longer owned by me and of quilts-in-progress, some of the interior studio shots, my studio being built, trees, color studies, things-in-a-row, some of the whirligigs, weaving and those of Sadie Chesrown.

### Jean Alexander Greenwald

Jean and Carol photographed the bulk of my quilts and some of my folk art collection in color. The two are from Seattle, Washington, and flew in with their equipment to live with me here on the farm while shooting my quilts. Unless identified, they took all photos in this book.

**Kevin Fitzsimons**, Columbus, Ohio, took the color photographs of LADY OF GUADALUPE III, MEXICAN WHEELS II and of me in my studio standing in front of MEXICAN WHEELS I. He also took the current black and white photos of me in my studio (front and back inside covers).

❖ (Right) A week's worth of ironing!

❖ (Below) Fabrics after being washed to remove excess dyes, dryed, ironed and folded. Ready to be used . . . the CONTENTS!

Both photographs by Nancy Crow.

# TABLE OF CONTENTS

# DEDICATED TO RACHEL ELIZABETH KENSETT CROW

I cannot begin this book without talking about my mother who was a huge influence in my life. I was the last of her eight children, born when she was 43 and my father was 48. All eight of us grew up in a highly creative and nurturing atmosphere . . . with no television! To give a sense of who she was and the richness of our environment, I have chosen excerpts from written accounts by each of my four sisters and three brothers beginning with the eldest and covering the time frame from 1920-1983. It is important to note that my mother's own father died when she was 12 years old, and her mother moved the family of four from Pennsylvania to New Concord, Ohio, where she opened a boarding house to support them all. The early teen years were evidently difficult for both my mother and her mother as portrayed here by my mother's brother, James Kensett. He wrote the following at age 88. James Kensett: "Our mother, Elizabeth Kensett, was of a slow deliberate temperament while Rachel was the opposite . . . quick, fast, impetuous in thinking and acting. This difference in temperament caused some incompatibility between daughter and mother. So in 1915 Rachel went off to live with Aunt Nan, mother's sister in Tacoma, Washington, for her junior year of high school. Rachel loved Aunt Nan as they were alike in actions and temperaments. Upon her return to New Concord, Ohio, (where our mother kept a boarding house), Rachel became well-liked by the young men at Muskingham College and dated often. This was all very worrisome to Mother. To make life easier, she sent Rachel off to Western College for Women, Oxford, Ohio, in 1917, where she finished her freshmen and sophomore years of college."

Before leaving for college, Mother had fallen deeply in love with Glenn Crow,

*❖ (Above) Rachel Elizabeth Kensett, 1917, when she was attending Western College for Women, Oxford, Ohio.*

*❖ (Far Right) Glenn Frank Crow in World War I uniform. Circa 1919.*

*❖ (Right) Boarding house where my mother spent her late childhood and high school years.*

❖ *(Below) Photo of Rachel Elizabeth Kensett in Tramp Art frame. She was 17 when the photo was taken in 1916.*

# RACHEL ELIZABETH KENSETT CROW

SEPTEMBER 4, 1899-NOVEMBER 7, 1984

a student at Muskingum College. He had come to New Concord from Loudonville, Ohio. While at Muskingum, he was drafted into World World I and sent to France. Upon his return two years later, he married Rachel Kensett on July 17, 1919. One year later, the first child of their eight children was born, with three more in rapid succession. There was a pause of eight years before the twins were born, and then another pause of eight years before my last brother and then I was born. Below is a photo of Mother and Father with the first four children when he worked as a mechanic to support his family. The photograph was taken around 1926.

and cold outer rooms. In the summer, an old-fashioned ice box presented her with a great deal of sour milk and rancid butter, plus a constantly overflowing drain basin on the back porch. Meanwhile, the year round, she washed clothes for us in an old wringer washer type Maytag and hung the clothes out to dry on the wire clothesline in the backyard. In the winter it was discouraging, I am sure, for Mother to bring the clothes in from the line all covered with soot and often frozen as hard as boards. She cooked every day on a gas kitchen stove which generated oil residues on every surface throughout the house that required several annual house cleanings of the walls and woodwork.

❖ *(Right) 1926 photo of (left to right) my father, Glenn Crow, my brother, David, my sister, Anne, my sister, Betty, my brother, Tom and my mother, Rachel.*

Thomas Seabury Crow (b. 1920): "I recall the unstinting devotion Mother gave during the first 10 years of my life from 1920-30. She performed a great deal of drudgery for our benefit while at the same time promoting a happy childhood for us (my two sisters and my younger brother). In the winter, she put up with a coal stove to heat the house which included pervasive dust from the ashes,

We even had gas light instead of electricity for several of my earlier years, which further compounded the problem. During this time, the the only thing that I remember that Mother did for her own pleasure was to play occasionally the old upright piano in the corner of the living room. At bedtime she would read children's stories to us and recite nursery rhymes so that we children gained a background in these cultural heritages that so many youngsters today seem to lack. All this time, as mother worked in the house, I remember we enjoyed playing in the neighborhood with our friends and never do I remember that mother was not happy for us to do so."

Rachel Elizabeth Crow Campochiaro (Betty) (b. 1921): "We lived in a frame house on Market Street in Loudonville, Ohio, during the 1920's and early 1930's. There was no plumbing and the house was lit by gas fixtures. Heat was provided by a small gas stove in the living room and an ugly coal stove in the dining room that was removed in the spring and set up again in the fall. Bathing and washing were done in the kitchen with water from a primed pump heated on the kitchen stove. Mother had to descend a steep flight of stairs to the backyard and hang the clothes on a line where they froze stiff in winter, then carry them back upstairs and iron them. The house was built on a hill and a dirt cellar and garage were on the lower level. The hill was perfect for sledding in winter. And because it was so steep, Dad did not use the garage much so we children, especially the boys, used it for a playroom.

❖ *(Left) Betty Crow on the left and Tom Crow on the right. Circa 1923.*
❖ *(Below) Tom Crow painting the word "Lincoln" on the car he and his brother, David, (sitting in the car) built from orange crates down in the garage below the house on Market Street. Forest Swank, a high school chum, is in the background. Circa 1928. Photograph by Glenn Crow.*

"We girls and our friends also played house in the damp cellar beyond. Because Mother liked to keep her children at home she encouraged the neighborhood kids to come to our house and often fed them cookies hot from the oven in the afternoons. We dug caves into the hill below our house, and when the lowlands flooded in spring and summer, we waded in the muddy water. Mother was a born gardener and an early riser so that she could work in her garden undisturbed. She loved to take us on nature walks and identified the plants and trees by their Latin names. She eagerly watched for birds, knew all their names and fed them regularly. She read books to us, a chapter at a time, when we were all in bed. We always had lots of books at home, most of them borrowed from the town library where we went as a matter of course. Tuesday was Dad's babysitting night when Mother went to Progress Club (a literary club), her one outlet away from the family. She was a voracious reader, and she made lifelong friends there. Dad, who could do anything with his hands, installed electricity, plumbing and a bathroom after the Loudonville town sewer system was installed. So life became easier by degrees. When the twins were born in 1933, we moved on to a larger house on another street and our lives changed, but I'll always remember the good times that Mother seemed to give us so effortlessly on Market Street. Looking back, I realize that her work must have been unending for she had no outside help and four children born to her in her first five years of marriage."

Anne Kensett Crow Gilleran (b. 1923): "Mother was paradoxical. In her 80's, on the phone, to me her voice was as young as a teenager's. She was alert and interested, ready to go. But in the evening she folded, asleep in her chair, for she was a morning person. Mother longed to be the person she was not. She seemed unaware of her virtues. Among the authentic marvels of my mother were the letters she wrote. I thought her penmanship was beautiful. I stared at her capital letters. How did she make them? Where did she learn how to do it? Who among us, especially her family, did not receive far more letters from her than she received from us? Not long ago, a cousin who lives on the West Coast, who had not seen Mother for years, said to me, "I always liked to go to Aunt Rachel's. I could do things at her house that I was never allowed to do at our home." And it is true; though she bemoaned the mess, she let us make it. The kitchen was often filled with children cooking, popping corn, making sticky popcorn balls, candy,

❖ (Right) David Crow on the left and Anne Crow on the right in wagon. Circa 1927.

cookies, doughnuts, catsup, root beer, and, once, even bottling homemade wine. The dining room table was covered with unfinished letters, sewing projects, books, childrens' homework, games, the day's mail, and then, it was all cleared away, covered with a tablecloth, and we ate a delicious meal together."

David Glenn Crow (b. 1925): "Her body grew old, but her outlook on life never did. She made plans at 80 as if she were 50, or maybe even 40. She was truly 'young at heart.' I also think she was a good judge of character; she found good traits in all those around her and expanded them with her love."

marvelous colors. How happy she was to have seen it. Always wanting to be in on whatever we were doing was one of her most endearing characteristics. Because she didn't want to be left out, Mother was not the first to say 'uncle.' She never complained. She was so pleased with the experiences she found on trips with her children. In Barcelona the architecture of Gaudi was a revelation to her. We decided at the last minute to go there. I'm glad we did. On the same trip we stayed at Brown's Hotel in London. That was fun for Mother too ... everything was so English ... Victorian rooms and formal tea. She always really liked that kind of thing. She was a grand companion."

❖ (Left) My father, Glenn Crow, with my twin sisters, Martha, on the left, and Mary on the right. 1934.

Martha Milliken Crow (b. 1933): "For years I have had an on-going conversation in my head with Mother – a silent dialogue that is hard to stop – 'Look at the – I can't wait to tell you about that. Mother, we must include this on our next trip. It will be such fun to . . . go to St. Chappelle.' In Paris she was so surprised and impressed with the towering stained glass windows of St. Chappelle. Somehow she'd never heard of the hidden-away Gothic chapel. I remember her joy in discovering its light and airy arches, its vast expanse of beautiful old glass, its

Mary Finley Crow (b. 1933): "In 1977, when I was staying in Cuernavaca, Mexico, I received a telegram at the school where I was studying Spanish. It said: Estoy aquí. Llámame. Mama. A telephone number in Mexico City followed. That telegram meant: I'm here. Call me. Mother. So I called and immediately took the bus down to Mexico City where I found Mother comfortable in an old, colonial-style hotel. She was then 77 and had for some time been having trouble getting around. She had very arthritic knees. However, that didn't stop her. We spent the day sight-seeing in Mexico City, and then we took the bus back to Guernavaca so she could visit that hilly but beautiful town and have dinner in the garden of one of the best restaurants, peacocks and pheasants strolling by, braziers burning, my old landlord using his courtly best Latin manners toasting Mother, Mother nodding and smiling, and me in the middle translating both directions. That sudden appearance in Mexico, the sense of adventure and the gameness, typify Mother. She loved to travel, and she loved adventure, a love that extended itself into other areas of her life and helped her to go on finding ways of opening herself and of growing. That was a wonderful gift she gave us . . . to be able to watch a parent grow old and yet grow young, to go on learning and re-learning. The willingness to be ready for what comes along, to try to grow even when growth is painful, the desire to hold the family together . . . these are some of the lessons Mother taught us."

ship that left my mother without the skills to deal with her suddenly changed life and the two children still at home . . . Nancy and me. I watched as depression began to wear her away until it seemed she would be destroyed. Finally, one day she began to fight back. She began to learn the skills she needed to compete in a new environment and to discard her Victorian female background. I watched as she began to develop her mind, let it absorb new ideas and experiences. I watched as she began to mold life to fit her the way she wanted. As I grew, I began to realize that not only was this person my mother, but that she had become my friend. Someone I loved, certainly, but also someone I respected, enjoyed, really liked! I began to lean back and look at this person and realize that I was really glad to know her. I will always remember her and remain joyful that she lived the life she did, and that I was part of it."

Andrew Nathaniel Crow (b. 1941): "My view of our mother was from a different point in time than that of my brothers and sisters. It really began when I was 14 and saw her devastated by the death of our father àt age 60 in 1955. It was the sudden end of a strong relation-

Nancy Morrison Crow (b. 1943): "I, too, like Andrew was strongly affected by the death of our father (I was age 12) and the subsequent emotional turmoil in our lives. Mother and Father were very much in love with one another and were always demonstrative in front of us. They represented a strong force in our lives. They took us on trips, on Sunday outings to Mohican State Forest, to art museums, to plays at Wooster College. Father loved art and bought art books. He also bought all of the oriental rugs we grew up with. Both he and Mother were amateur photographers and won many awards. He kept a dark room in the basement. Both he and Mother were excellent with their hands. And they believed fiercely in education and determined that all eight of their children would go to college, hopefully liberal arts colleges. Father thought it was most important to have a liberal arts education first before specializing.

"I believe my father was sensitive about helping out with the family, the children, because his own mother, Norah Crow, was left to take care of two tiny children by herself. He grew up seeing

❖ (Right) Nancy and Andrew Crow in front of the Crow home in Loudonville, Ohio, 1948.

how hard she had to work. And he felt sympathetic towards her. He also had to take jobs while a young teenager and at one time was apprenticed to a Loudonville tailor. He learned to sew well enough to make winter coats for his little daughters during the Depression when there was no money to buy clothes. Mother, alas, would later sit at her Singer and throw her hands up in despair as the sewing machine was forever an enigma to her. She never could teach me how to use it. I learned in 4-H when I was 11 or 12 years old.

"Mother had qualities that I realize now were 'outstanding.' She was forthright. Never playing games with her emotions. We always knew exactly how she felt about everything. If she was angry she told us. If sad or unhappy, likewise. She was affectionate with us, full of praise, always interested in everything we were doing. She never said 'shut-up' to any of us as she felt the expression far too insulting. She made me feel as though I could do anything. 'That's wonderful' was a phrase applied often. Her enthusiasm was contagious as was her laughter. One wanted to be with her. She was forever sending clippings from magazines and newspapers that she thought would be of interest, and she called on the phone nearly every other day.

"In 1961 when I began my freshman year at Ohio State University in Columbus, Ohio, Mother at age 62 decided she wanted to go back to school and finish those last two years. So she too enrolled at Ohio State and drove 160 miles back and forth everyday until she finished. She graduated in 1963, taught one year of grade school and was then retired!

"I will always remember my mother and my father as very good human beings."

❖ (Left) Rachel Kensett Crow in 1982 at the age of 83.

# FOREWORD

## By Jean Robertson

Nancy Crow works in a large studio at the end of a long lane on an isolated farm in central Ohio. In her studio on open shelves are myriad piles of fabrics, which shock the eyes with their bold patterns and strong colors: alizarin crimson, cobalt blue, cadmium orange, lemon yellow, viridian green and on and on through every imaginable tone. In her studio are hundreds of books about painting, sculpture, textiles, folk art, writing, gardening and philosophy. In her studio pinned to walls are two or three quilts in progress, each from a different series with its own set of shapes.

Life as an artist on an Ohio farm has been both hard and liberating. Crow, a gregarious, articulate woman, has had to confront loneliness and learn to look inward for inspiration and strength. The same isolation has promoted boundless freedom of expression. No one looks over the artist's shoulder as she experiments with shapes, values and colors, creating quilt tops of the utmost modernity. Crow works alone, her imagination fired by the piles of fabrics, as if the colors were emitting electrical charges, and by images and passages in her well-thumbed books.

Crow came relatively late to piecing fabric as her medium. She studied ceramics and weaving in art school (at the Ohio State University), then devoted six more years to tapestry weaving. She has only been making quilts seriously since 1979. Her advancement, as this book documents, has been rapid.

Crow loves the feel of fine fabrics and certainly her quilts have a tactile richness and sculptural body impossible to create in paint. But the soul of Crow's work is color. Each new quilt is a drama of color directly creating form. Crow possesses an instinctive eye for color harmonies and rhythms, the equivalent of perfect pitch in music. Her virtuosity as a colorist enables her unerringly to play light, medium and dark tones against one another to orchestrate subtle optical effects: tensions between positive and negative space; illusions of depth and shifting planes; the impression of light emanating from within the fabric. In making quilts, Crow says, she experiences "the absolute joy of trying new colors with other colors."*

Crow is always working at the edge of what she knows, experimenting, taking new risks. Many artists pare down their vocabulary as they develop. Crow is evolving towards greater complexity. She says, "I try all the time to use more colors. One of my goals is to have hundreds and hundreds of colors within one quilt." Like mosaic, millefiore glass, stained glass, tapestry and collage, her compositions transform heterogeneous, potentially clashing elements into one harmonious surface. Each quilt is a self-contained world, perfect unto itself.

Does Crow know that she is considered among the most innovative of contemporary quilt artists, that her reputation and influence extend from coast to coast? When you meet her she talks more about her struggles than her achievements. One imagines Crow, a fiercely self-disciplined artist, alone in her studio each day pushing herself into a state of incredible concentration and visual awareness where she is able first to gather into her mind's eye all the intricate details of a stunningly complex pattern, then mentally to shuffle shapes and colors so that the kaleidoscope locks into an evermore flawless arrangement. Time permeates Crow's quilts, formed like spider's webs over days and weeks of single-minded effort. Yet the struggle is not apparent in the finished quilt, where every square inch appears complete, inevitable, necessary to the whole.

Crow struggles emotionally as well as aesthetically. She is passionate. She is truthful. She is sensitive, tenacious, vibrant and complicated. The geometric clarity of her compositions is hard-won, the result of harnessing strong emotions, of replacing emotional turmoil with artistic order. The complexity of her designs echoes the complexity of her emotional life.

Crow knows much about formal elements like shape, pattern and color as well as how to handle fabric. But she does not make quilts to demonstrate technical ability. Her work is grounded in her need to honestly examine and express her own feelings: loneliness, sorrow, depression, anger, joy and hope. The BITTERSWEET series of 22 quilts ("they came out like a torrent") coincided with a three-year period of rapid artistic and personal change, kindled by her loneliness and depression after first moving to the farm in 1979. Courageously looking inward, Crow realized she had depended entirely on others for fulfillment; now she had to accept responsibility for her own happiness. According to Crow, in that series a block "represents me and shows me changing from quilt to quilt to quilt as I grow and mature." The artist you meet today is strong, self-reliant, thoughtful, focused and passionate but clear.

Crow says she feels wholeness and sanity when she works. Her talent is to move from the painfully personal to the resolution of aesthetic order. Fueled by a mood of emotional intensity, she arrives at structures where all the pieces harmonize. Thus during the one and a half years she spent with her dying mother, Crow translated her grief into the red and blue and black geometries of the PASSION series of quilts (1983-1984), asserting her faith in artistic balance as a counter to the chaos and pain of the world. Likewise intense joy can drive her, as in the MEXICAN WHEELS series which is a current preoccupation. "I'm trying to release something within myself," she says, "I'm trying to work into more freedom."

Crow prefers working in a series, one quilt giving birth to the next. The discipline of creating within constants established for a series channels and ultimately liberates her imagination. Crow gains confidence varying colors, for example, if she knows the basic shapes are fixed. In fact, her inventions usually grow more daring later in a series. In the first or second quilt, she may be tentative, exploratory, still learning the new shapes. Finally she becomes fluent in the new language, able to express ideas without premeditation. Her process may be a holdover from her studies in ceramics, when she was influenced by the Japanese attitude that repetition leads to perfection, that "you take an idea, and you do it over and over and over until you get past that initial idea and it starts to be spontaneous."

Quilting extends back to the ancient Chinese, who quilted layers of cloth to make warm winter garments. The technique spread to the Arabs, then to the Europeans, who adapted the technique to make bed coverings. In America, patchwork flourished in the colonial era as a means of making new clothing and bed quilts out of precious scraps of scarce fabric. Quilting remained popular until the late 19th century when bed coverings made on power looms replaced handmade quilts in most households. Today the medium is enjoying a revival and a redefinition in the hands of artists like Nancy Crow.

Normally, we only have the opportunity to see a few of Crow's quilts at once, when we visit an exhibition. This book provides a special opportunity to view a decade of work in depth, and to begin to understand how time and experience have shaped Crow's creativity. It is fitting that the book presents the artist's words beside her work. Her quilts embody insights about art and life achieved through enormous effort; her words help us to fathom her discoveries.

*All quotations are from an interview the author conducted with Nancy Crow at the artist's studio on August 17, 1988.

Jean Robertson
236 Van Buren Blvd.
Terra Haute, IN 47803
Tel.: (812)234-3485

# INTRODUCTION

I find it very curious that I am writing the "Introduction" last. All along I thought I was procrastinating, but now I realize that it was important to me to see "how the book would go together" before I could write all the thoughts that might make it more understandable.

The Dedication: To start with, I felt I both wanted and needed to write an in-depth "Dedication" because my family has been such a powerful influence on my life. Both my mother and my father were so generous in spirit, ideas and affection. As children, we were allowed full access to daydreams and fantasies. We were given lots of time to play. There was no television lulling us into a stupor hour after hour. We were encouraged to develop our own visual perceptions. I remember the hours spent in the empty lot across from our yard where weeds were allowed to grow quite tall, taller than I. We children fell on them and crushed them down flat in an effort to carve out a spot for our pretend house. I was, and am, a visual-learner, responding so strongly to my surroundings. I remember the chicken coops that nearly everyone had in their backyards when I was a child. These coops were so mysterious to me with their little doors where one by one, white or brown birds would walk out. I made daily trips from one chicken coop to another just to see what was going on that day. Each chicken yard had its own personality. The chickens dug or scratched out all manner of holes in the dirt and I loved to see what "garbage" had been thrown out and to see the chickens pecking through it. I loved walking through the alleys to see what plants were blooming in the forgotten corners of backyards. I remember a marvelous clump of orange Chinese lanterns that I went looking for in late summer every year. I thought them very mysterious. And so too the asparagus popping up

every spring! It was miraculous to me. I roller-skated on sidewalks long heaved up by the bulging roots of ancient sugar maples lining the streets. But I incorporated the heaving walks into a pretend story about going up hill and down to reach my long lost home. It was a challenge to skate up and down and miss falling in the cracks. On the way home I pretended I was a "star skater" with long beautiful legs. And when I was old enough, I relished those relentless games of canasta, parcheesi or monopoly going on at one of three houses in the neighborhood, always with the same five or six kids. We were all very competitive. None of us had the huge number of toys that children have today. We relied on imagination for much of our playing, making up games such as "cowboys and Indians." After getting my first cowboy boots, I remember days and days spent riding my pretend horse down our steep hill and over to a steeper hill behind the house where I would sit and watch cloud patterns till I was tired. Then I would ride my "horse" back home hoping everyone would notice my new cowboy boots.

Historical Background: I have begun this book with a very short historical background of Ashland County and the small town, Loudonville, where I grew up. I have also included wonderful old

❖ (Right) Nancy Crow at age 7 sitting in the backyard. Loudonville, Ohio. Circa 1950.

quilts found in families still living in Ashland County and one made by my grandmother, Norah Crow.

First Quilts: I have described those early quilts that I made while still giving most of my time to tapestry weaving.

Quilts (1976-1979): I discuss the quilts I made from 1976-1979. It was during this period that my love of quiltmaking grew strong enough to make me decide to give up tapestry weaving and become a full-time quiltmaker.

Move To The Farm (1979): I describe the ramifications of moving to our farm where my husband, John Stitzlein and our two sons, Nathaniel and Matthew and I live now. This move had a profound impact on my quiltmaking and helped me to become focused.

Building A Studio (1980-1984) and Addition (1986-1987): I outline my decision to build a studio of my own and then later to enlarge it with an addition.

Quilts (1980-1988): I cover the quilts made from 1980-1988, year by year. My production has at times been uneven depending upon outside events which I discuss. But I have also come to realize that my production has slowed down in direct proportion to the increasing complexity within my quilts. And I hold the conviction that a quilt cannot be hurried. Solutions come in their own good time. And when solutions are contrived or hurried up, the quilt often fails. To be successful, it seems to me a quilt must "glow from an inner spirit."

As I wrote about the newest quilts from 1986-88, I included many photographs of "quilts-in-progress" to show my working methods. I do not plan my quilts out on paper before making them. I usually start with a vague idea and work intuitively at the wall, pinning up fabric shapes, trying colors, paying attention to the overall composition as it develops, discarding anything that does not work. I believe in trial and error. I am not afraid to waste fabric. I often start with traditional blocks when beginning a new quilt. The familiarity with the traditional shapes seems to give me the "license" I need to be inventive in some contrary way. For instance, I loved "blowing up" the Double Wedding Ring block to such a large size that in a sense it abstracted the whole design and made it nearly overwhelming visually. I did this as a "direct slap" at all those old Double Wedding Ring quilts made of left-over, washed-out scraps. As a young woman I hated those ugly quilts. They were totally uninspiring and maybe that is why quiltmaking did not interest me until much later.

Sadie Chesrown (1898-1986): I gave my dear friend, Sadie Chesrown, a chapter of her own because she represents to me "true originality." She was eccentric. And I love the idea of being eccentric because it sustains the assumption that one does not care what others think about her or him. Therefore that person operates in a state of freedom. So much of art suffers today because the maker is often far too aware of what others want or expect or will buy. But Sadie was an "original." She made a strong statement about who she was simply by the life she led.

Influences: Lastly, I have covered the other "Influences" in my life, influences that have contributed to my work.

Things-In-A-Row: I have thought and thought about why I have always been so drawn to "Things-In-A-Row" . . . a very strong graphic attraction for me. One of my earliest recollections is of being "relegated" to the basement by my teenage twin sisters, Mary and Martha, whenever I wanted to play my 78 rpm records. They had a life of their own that did not include me, and they did not want to hear my music when they were playing in the living room. So I carried the old record player down to the section of the basement where Mother kept all her canned goods, all those jars of vegetables she put up every summer. I set up my record player on an old wooden bench and usually put on a broadway musical such as "Diamonds are a Girl's Best Friend." I would work out elaborate dance routines, memorize all the words to the music, and fling myself all around the small room with its concrete floor, block walls and bare light bulb burning overhead. When I was sufficiently carried away, I remember running my eyes back and forth across the rows of canned beans, tomatoes and cucumbers. Jars of color and pattern all lined up on the shelves, shelf after shelf. The light from the bulb overhead caused the jars to throw shadows that formed more patterning. It was a mysterious world down in that old cellar until I got old enough and tall enough to realize there were cobwebs hanging from the rafters, that it was too dark and that I actually hated the basement. It smelled funny!

I also found Things-In-A-Row hidden under a pile of folded clothes in the hall closet where we hung our coats. There was a shelf built into the wall behind the coats, and Mother loved to hide things there thinking I would never know. But

I always found the candies. For a time, Dad received each year a gift of boxes of special candies from a customer in the Middle East. By the time I was born, my father was vice president of sales at the Flxible Company in Loudonville. The Flxible Company made city buses, and Dad had many customers outside the United States so he received gifts. And these candies were special, chewy, with pecans inside, and a thin white papery coating. Little rectangles all lined up just waiting to be eaten. I was fixated on those candies. Mother always wondered how the candy kept disappearing so rapidly! She abhorred the eating of sweets while Dad relished them and I . . . I had no intention of letting that candy grow stale!

Mother always read to my brother, Andrew, and me just before we went to bed. My favorite books were *Katy and the Big Snow, Mike Mulligan and His Steam Shovel* and *Calico, The Wonder Horse*, all by Virginia Lee Burton who also illustrated the books. In *Katy and The Big Snow*, there were wonderful borders around each page. The borders consisted of drawings of Things-In-A-Row, in progression, changing from one to another. These Things-In-A-Row were like puzzles to me . . . I had to study them to see how each differed from the one before. I was

❖ *(Right) Page 1 from the children's book* Katy and the Big Snow *by Virginia Lee Burton, Houghton Mifflin, Co., Boston. (Both the drawings and the story are by Virginia Lee Burton.)*

entranced by the illustrations and never tired of looking at the book, I loved all the details. (Refer to photograph on preceding page).

And then there was the Loudonville Free Street Fair that I attended every October. Mother gave Andy and me each 50¢. That was it for each day. No more. Well, even back then, 50¢ did not go very far especially if one wanted to eat "that awful fair food," go on rides, and of course, play those "horrible games that are such a waste of money!" But I was intrigued by the bottles lined up and hoped I could throw a wooden ring over the neck of at least one. And how about those stuffed creatures lined up in rows just waiting to be knocked over by a well-aimed ball. Maybe I could win a teddy bear. I was like a waif running all around the fair in my excitement. Poor Grandmother Kensett! (Mother's mother). Andy and I would run over to her house and beg for more money. She had hardly any to give, but she always gave us something. She was 85 at the time.

Doors: I was intrigued by the door in a book titled *The Secret Garden*. There was risk involved for whoever opened it but a paradise behind.

And then there was the tiny door up in my bedroom that I was scared to open for such a long time. I feared whatever spirits might be behind. It was actually the door to a crawl space where a bunch of junk was stored.

And maybe it was the emphasis on the door to my parents' bedroom which we were never allowed to enter without permission.

Or the door at the bottom of the steps leading into the living room. The door at which I spent many, many nights crying, standing there, looking into the brightly lit room where Mother and Father sat reading, the room where I was not allowed because I was supposed to be in bed upstairs. It was a French door with many panes of glass bound by thick fancy woodwork. I would trace all around the inside of the frames with my fingers, window pane after window pane, while

❖ *(Below): Bottle game at the fair. Photograph by Nancy Crow.*

waiting hopefully for permission to open the door. I didn't want to stay upstairs in that dark bedroom with that spooky little door that I could see from my bed. And besides I was never sure who was lying under my bed ready to scare me. The house was always creaking and making funny noises at night. It seemed eternity before I outgrew this stage.

Color: I have only a few theories about color. One is connected to the oriental rugs that covered the wood floors in our house. Whenever I was sick as a child, I got the living room couch as my very "own sanctuary." Mother waited on me as though I were a princess. As I listened to the radio lying on the couch, I would study the meandering patterns of flowers and birds. I would notice where the yarns changed colors.

As for yellow which I love, I remember two things. There was a large collection of *National Geographic* magazines on the bookshelf. One couldn't help but notice that impact of yellow on a regular daily basis.

And then, Andy and I had an "unusual yellow experience" at Grandmother Kensett's house. When the two of us would visit her, she always let us knead her plastic bag of margarine. It was white when she bought it at the store but there was a cube of colorant inside the bag. By kneading the bag over and over thoroughly, we could work in the yellow color until it looked like butter. That was always a miracle of some sort to me even if it did taste terrible!

And, of course, there were always the wonderful flowers my mother raised in her annual and perennial beds. She had a "life of her own" when it came to her gardening. One could feel her intensity. When one is small, any bud opening into color is always a surprise, a treat.

Tramp Art and Whirligigs: I love both since they are made up of bits and pieces.

Artifacts: My oldest sister, Betty, was a command librarian for the Air Force stationed first in West Germany and then England. When she brought home gifts for each of us, she brought home "exotic" things, wonderful things, full of good design, well made, that made me aware of other countries' artistic heritages.

Baskets: I began collecting baskets as a teenager, and I have a very extensive collection now that includes baskets from all over the world. I even had a basket shop for two years while we lived in Athens, Ohio. I carried excellent quality, old and new, but I discovered the public wanted baskets for $6.00 or less. The public never understood the skill, the love, the intelligence that goes into basket-making. So I closed shop and ended up with a magnificent collection.

I also became interested in finding out who the native basket makers were in Ohio and if any were still living. I found three and documented by photographs two of them.

Trees: Trees have always been one of the strongest influences in my life. A mature tree is one of the boldest graphic impressions that any human will witness in his daily life. During my childhood, I grew older along with the Norway maple that was planted just outside the window of my second-floor bedroom. Each year it got taller, and I got taller. During the winter, its branches formed black silhouettes against the sky. I lay in bed staring out the window up through the branches to the night sky. There were always new configurations of the branches, new patterns being formed by slight breezes or heavy winds. I have always felt sorry for children who did not grow up with a large tree outside their bedroom window. The tree becomes a companion, a form of security. And for me, it was my first exposure to art. By day it was sculpture; by night, flat patterning against the sky. And it was kinetic besides!

My father gave my brother, Andy, and me the job of watering two 18-foot tall pin oaks that he had had moved to our house in town from the farm. We watched Dad carefully ridge up the soil around each tree in a circle the diameter of which was about six feet. He showed us how to drape the garden hose over the ridge and let the water run until it was level with the top of the ridge. We were so young at the time that to Andy and me it was incredible to see this gooey, muddy mess forming. We pretended we had a tiny lake, and we floated our boats and stuck sticks into the water till we hit bottom, pretending that the lake was very, very deep! Each week we did Dad's bidding; we dragged out the hose, turned on the water and filled our own two lakes again. I was seven when I was given this task and I never really understood at the time why it was so important to keep watering those trees with so much water. But it forged an intimacy with trees that has affected me ever since.

Near the end of this book you will see photographs of a wild cherry tree that stands in the fence row between our farm and the neighbor's. The tree is on his side of the fence so it belongs to him. I can see "That Tree" from anywhere on the farm because it is so tall. It has been an anchor to me through nine years of emotions. I have photographed the tree endlessly during every season. And it endures. Through sunny days, snowy weather. Insecticides and herbicides blow at it. Branches break. Branches are cut off, but it is still majestic. It endures and that is a lesson in itself.

❖ *(Below) Glenn Crow, my father, standing in the woods with his camera. He loved trees and was an amateur photographer. Circa 1950.*

# HISTORICAL BACKGROUND

I was born in and grew up in the small town of Loudonville, Ohio, in Ashland County which is located in the north central part of the state. This area is called the "Little Switzerland of Ohio" due to steep rolling hills and many forested acres. It is extraordinarily beautiful farm country not far from the huge Amish settlements of Homes County. The Mohican Indians roamed the countryside during the 1700's after being driven from their lands in Rhode Island and Connecticut. The Mohican River winds near Loudonville and the Mohican State Forest is located about 5 miles from the southern edge of this town of 2,800.

I chose to begin my book with outstanding examples of quilts owned by families living in Ashland County. I deliberately selected quilts with patterns that have intrigued me almost from the beginning of my own quiltmaking. Due to the extensive leg-work of the Ohio Quilt Research Project I was able to locate rapidly those quilts that I wanted to have photographed and an all-day photography session was set up at the Cleo Redd Fisher Museum in Loudonville.

One of the quilts photographed that day was an incredible embroidered fan quilt from the permanent collection of the museum. It had been pieced out of earthen-colored woolens, and names had been embroidered on the spokes of the fans. I was told it had been a fund-raising quilt, circa 1900, and that for 10¢, one could have one's name embroidered on the quilt. I looked closer only to discover with great excitement that my father's name, Glenn Frank Crow, was there. Then I found his brother's name and his mother's and then his grandfather's and on and on. I felt a peculiar sense of energy pass from the quilt to me. Here I was – in May 1988 – in my hometown where I no longer have any living relatives, staring at a quilt containing the names of my father's family who had lived in the area since 1830. It was very emotional for me because I never knew any of these people except my father. My sense of them had come from his spoken and written reminiscences.

No one in my family had ever mentioned this quilt, so I feel I am the first to have seen it.

I will start with this FAN QUILT and then with a quilt made by my paternal grandmother, Norah Bird Crow. After that, I have included a selection of quilts from Ashland County families.

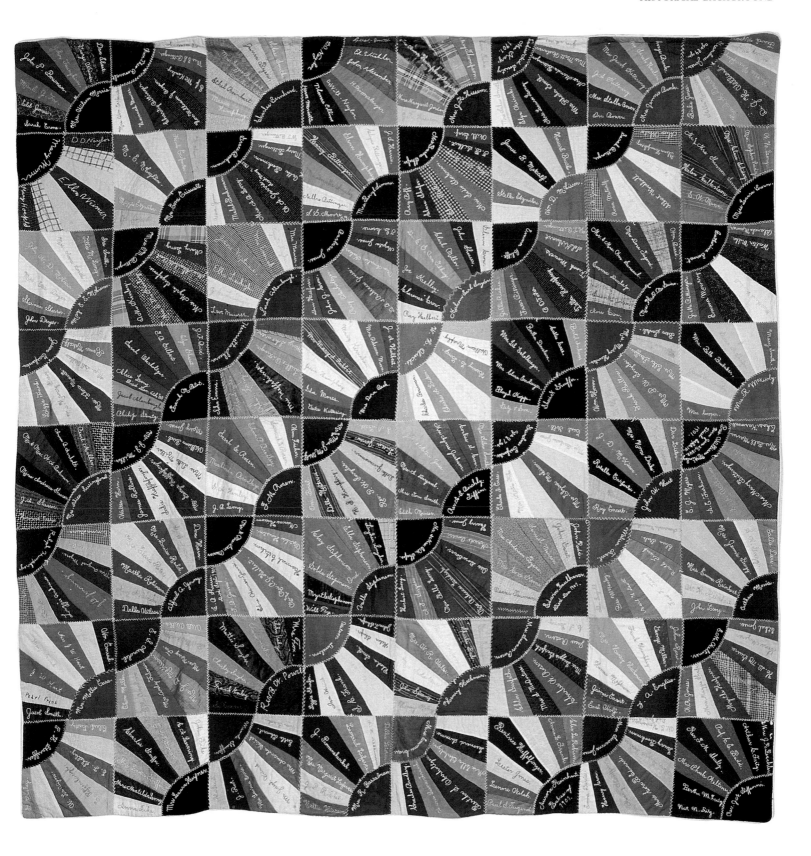

❖ *(Above) EMBROIDERED FAN QUILT, circa 1900, (74" x 77"), Ashland County, Ohio. Collection of the Cleo Redd Fisher Museum, Loudonville, Ohio.*

❖ *(Opposite right) Detail of FAN QUILT. Circa 1900.*

❖ *(Below) My paternal grandmother, Norah Bird Crow, with her two sons, Glenn Frank Crow, on the right, and Clarence Crow, on the left.*

Family names found in this quilt include:

Norah Bird Crow
Cameron Crow
Glenn Frank Crow
Clarence Crow
Sparks Bird, Sr.
Sparks Bird, Jr.

As I study the photograph of Grandmother Norah Bird Crow, I see a strong face, beautiful hands and a sense of determination. By the time this photo was taken, she was already a single mother raising two sons by herself. Norah was born in Ashland County, Ohio, in 1869, and married Cameron Crow who either was murdered or ran away while transporting a large sum of money for a local bank. No one ever knew. I did find a bundle of letters written to Norah by Cameron during 1899 in which he repeats the refrain from letter to letter that he is sorry they are so poor, and she deserves more. I found no letters of hers in reply so I have no idea of her feelings.

❖ *(Opposite page) NORAH'S QUILT, circa 1900, (70" x 78"), hand pieced and hand quilted by Norah Bird Crow. There is no batting since it is a summer quilt.*

❖ *(Below) Detail of NORAH'S QUILT.*

I have been told that Norah supported herself and her two sons by cleaning houses for other families and by taking in washing. Meantime she managed to create a wonderful environment of her own. My eldest sister, Betty, remembers Norah's house as being interesting with the quilting frame often set up in the living room . . . and that Grandmother made huge sugar cookies for them to eat!

So the interest in quiltmaking seems to have come solely from my father's side of the family, namely from Norah. By the time I was aware there were any old quilts left in our family, Norah had been dead 50 years. Mother gave me both of her quilts, one of which I have included. I find it sad that there is no record of how she felt about her life, her dreams, her quiltmaking, and that all her quilts have been used up except the two that I have. Or is it sad . . . since they were made to be used?

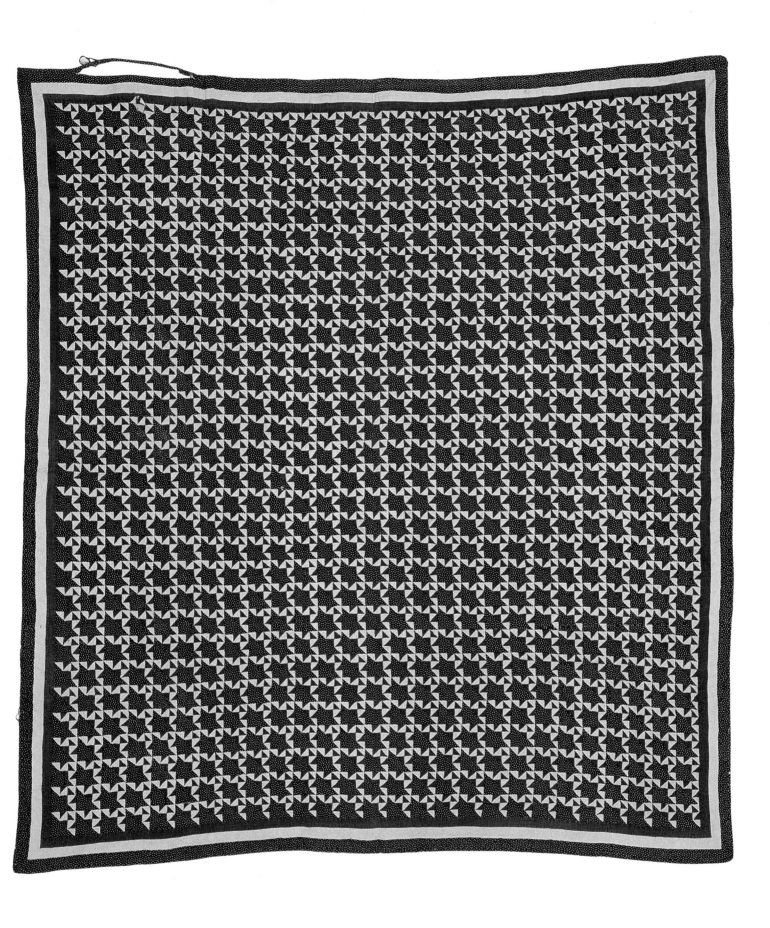

❖ *(Opposite page) LOG CABIN, circa 1885-90, (64" x 73"), cottons, pieced and hand quilted by Anne Smalley Harris, Ashland County, Ohio. Collection of Ann Shaffer.*

❖ *(Right) Detail of LOG CABIN by Anne Smalley Harris.*

❖ *(Below) STREAK O' LIGHTENING LOG CABIN, circa 1870, (71½" x 71"), cotton, silk and wool, hand pieced and quilted by Rachel Stickle Thome, Holmes County, Ohio. Collection of Lavern Pennell, Ashland County, Ohio.*

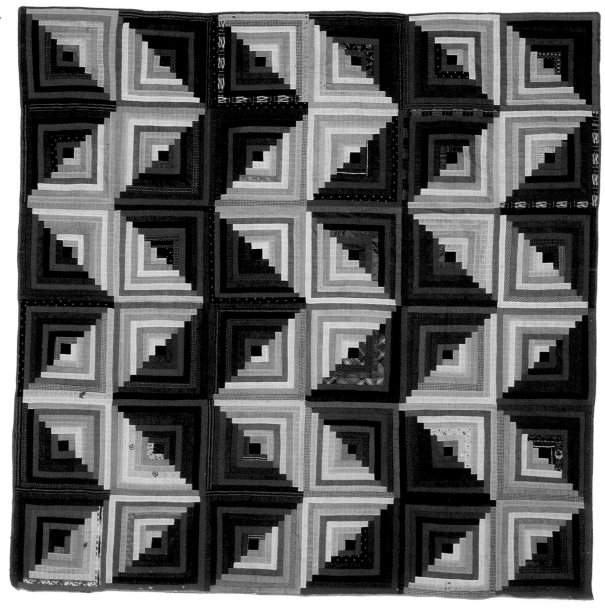

❖ *(Below) LOG CABIN in Court House Steps pattern, circa 1788, (80" x 82"), pieced by Permelia Davis Hickman and her sister, Sally Hawes.*

The LOG CABIN below was made of fine woolens that were freely cut and freely sewn together. No batting was used nor was there any quilting. Although the quilt was actually made in Harrison County, Indiana, it remains with family in Ashland County, Ohio. Collection of Wilma Kirkpatrick.

❖ (Left) CRAZY
STAR QUILT, circa
1900, (42" x 65"),
pieced by Elphred
Kyler Garn, Jer-
omesville, Ashland
County, Ohio.
Made of velvets
and silks.
Collection of
Millicent
Alexander Kyler,
Ashland County,
Ohio.

❖ (Opposite page) STRIPED STAR, circa 1900, (78" x 78"), pieced and knotted by Elphred Kyler Garn who was in her late 30's when she made this quilt. Cottons, excellent condition. It was kept in a cupboard with tobacco leaves. Collection of Millicent Alexander Kyler, Ashland Co., Ohio.

❖ (Above left) Detail of STRIPED STAR.

❖ (Above) Back of STRIPED STAR.

❖ (Left) LONE STAR, circa 1900, (85" x 85"), pieced by Rosa Deakins. Rosa pieced this vivid quilt for her Mother, Sara Jane Bird, who was losing her eyesight. She never quilted this top because she was busy caring for Sara. Collection of Olive Augenstein, Ashland Co., Ohio.

Jennie Harris Doerrer, born in 1885, who made the quilt below, was always interested in sewing and found it a challenge to find new ways to use up scraps of fabric. Her PHILADELPHIA PAVEMENT is made of scraps left over from sewing clothes for her family.

She also made many hooked rugs using burlap as a backing with her own hand-drawn motifs. She always had some sort of handwork in progress.

❖ (Above) Detail of PHILADELPHIA PAVEMENT.

❖ (Right) PHILADELPHIA PAVEMENT, circa 1930, (90" x 90"), pieced and quilted by Jennie Harris Doerrer, mother of Ann Shaffer. Collection of Ann Shaffer, Ashland County, Ohio.

❖ (Above) CRAZY SAWTOOTH, pre-1900, (74" x 74"), pieced and quilted by Amanda Workman Fulmer. Collection of Doris Strang, Ashland County, Ohio. Amanda was the grandmother of Doris Strang.

❖ *(Above) TURKEY TRACKS WITH SWAGS AND TASSEL BORDER, circa 1850, (73" x 83"), maker unknown, collection of Elnora Snyder, Ashland County, Ohio.*

The above applique quilt is made of cottons. When it was found, it was folded and being used as a pad between springs and mattress on a day bed.

❖ *(Above) FLORAL DISPLAY, circa 1868, (85" x 85"), applique and trapunto, made by Jane Ann Richard. Collection of Vivian May, Richland County, Ohio.*

❖ *(Above) Detail.*

❖ *(Right) NEW YORK BEAUTY WITH MARINER'S COMPASS, pieced and hand quilted by Mary Elizabeth Duncan, Lash, Cochocton County, Ohio, 1869. Collection of David Leckrone, Ashland County, Ohio.*

Around the border are pieced the words, LAVADA IDELLA LASH, BORN NOV. THE 9, 1869. Lavada's mother, Mary Elizabeth Duncan Lash, (1850-1918), pieced this quilt when she was 19 years old to commemorate Lavada's date of birth. Lavada was the first of twelve children.

David Leckrone, 24 years old, first knew of this quilt by his great-great grandmother when his Grandmother Leckrone's household goods were auctioned off several years ago. This quilt was found at the bottom of a box at the time of the auction. No one in the family knew it existed. "Because the design caught his eye and because it was made by his own relative," David bid until the quilt was his. The name around the border is that of his great-grandmother!

❖ *(Above) KANSAS TROUBLES, circa 1880, pieced and hand quilted by Arminda Heichel Stafford, Ashland County, Ohio.*

Arminda Heichel Stafford, (1856-1941), lived her entire life in Mohican Township, Ashland County, and was a descendant of the Pennsylvania Dutch who emigrated from Western Pennsylvania to Ohio in 1833.

Arminda worked by the light of a kerosene lamp and was known for her quilting, crewel embroidery, crocheting and tatting. She was a very conscientious person. It is believed that she made this quilt before she married in 1882. The quilt is now owned by her grandson, William J. Stafford and his wife, Maxine E. Stafford, Ashland County, Ohio. It is in excellent condition and is kept on display.

Mr. and Mrs. Walter A. Luce of Loudonville, Ohio, purchased this quilt in Tuscarawas County, Ohio. Although they do not know the maker or the date it was made, the quilt appears to be a version of the GREEK CROSS pattern.

❖ *(Below) GREEK CROSS, date and maker unknown.*

# FIRST QUILTS (1971-1975)

Chronology of where I have lived:

❖ (Opposite page) RED AND BLACK CROSSES, 1970-71, (64" x 78"), ©Nancy Crow, hand pieced and appliqued by Rachel Kensett Crow and Nancy Crow. All cottons.

In October 1969, my husband, John Stitzlein, and I left for Porto Alegre, Brazil, located in the most southern part of the country. We had both finished master's programs at Ohio State University. As part of his doctoral degree in agricultural economics, John would be doing research on the impact of mechanization on agriculture in rural Brazil. We lived there for 1½ years.

I took along my 45" floor loom and yarns, sewing machine and fabrics. My plan was to develop my weaving as much as possible while absorbing Brazilian culture. I also wanted to make a simple quilt to use. Before leaving I had designed a block and went shopping for fabrics. I chose only a few colors . . . black, red, white, yellow and some striped fabric. I planned to alternate 9-patch blocks with blocks of appliqued crosses.

I was three months pregnant with my first child when we left for Brazil and just before Nathaniel was born in March 1970, my mother, Rachel Crow, flew down to live with us for six months. She came to help out with the new baby, but instead I talked her into working on my quilt. It was she who did most of the applique and the piecing.

After we returned to the United States, I added the wide red border thinking that would make the quilt look "more modern." I do not remember now who hand quilted it. Nor do I remember ever being very excited about the quilt. I do know that I did not understand how to calculate how many blocks would be needed because I still have a whole stack of left-over blocks put away in a box. Enough to make one more quilt.

The quilt has had severe use on the children's beds and is now quite faded and tattered. Looking at it, I can't help musing about my limited color usage except that most quilts I had seen at that time had only two or three colors in them. And I must have accepted that that was the way quilts were made.

This is the only quilt on which my mother worked with me.

Before moving from Cambridge Ohio, (1972-1974), to Athens, Ohio, (1974-1979), I wove a huge 9' x 12' rag rug. Like my limited notion of what quilts were, my idea of rag rugs was of muddied colors due to the uninspired use of left-over clothing. Rag rugs were not for inspiration but for practicality! Using up scraps was more important than creating artworks!

So I decided I would make an "IN-SPIRED RAG RUG" and knock a hole in the common perception of rag rugs. As luck would have it, the local Goodwill was selling wool skirts at 2/15¢.

I remember an abundance of skirts hanging from racks and piled in huge boxes. I leaned over the edge of a box and worked my way to the bottom, pulling out all the pleated skirts thinking they contained more yardage. I concentrated on finding black, red, blue, green and white skirts. Only wool ones. When I got home with my carload, I put the skirts into piles by color and ripped out zippers, waistband and hems. I washed the skirts in hot water and dried them in the dryer to "felt" the wool, making it thicker. I also dyed some of the white skirts in various shades of yellow. Then I cut the skirts into 1" strips and rolled them into balls. I dressed my old Union loom with linen warp and proceeded to make the rug in five parts. As I wove the parts, I let the colors work in "hit-or-miss" as in typical rag rug fashion. But the big difference was my use of tapestry techniques to make diagonal lines and shapes. All the blues represent all the different blue skirts I found. The same for the reds, the blacks, the greens and the various shades of white.

After weaving the five different strips, each 12 ft. long, I whip-stitched the strips together side by side. John and I then rolled the rug up and took it north to his father's farm to photograph it on the side of the huge barn there.

This rug has never been used and still remains rolled-up in my studio. Not too practical, eh?!

It weighs an absolute ton. I never thought all those skirts would weigh so heavy. And it is very thick.

❖ (Above) Nancy Crow standing beside 9' x 12' rag rug she wove in 1974. Photo by John Stitzlein. ©Nancy Crow.

❖ (Right) Close-up of 9' x 12' rag rug. ©Nancy Crow.

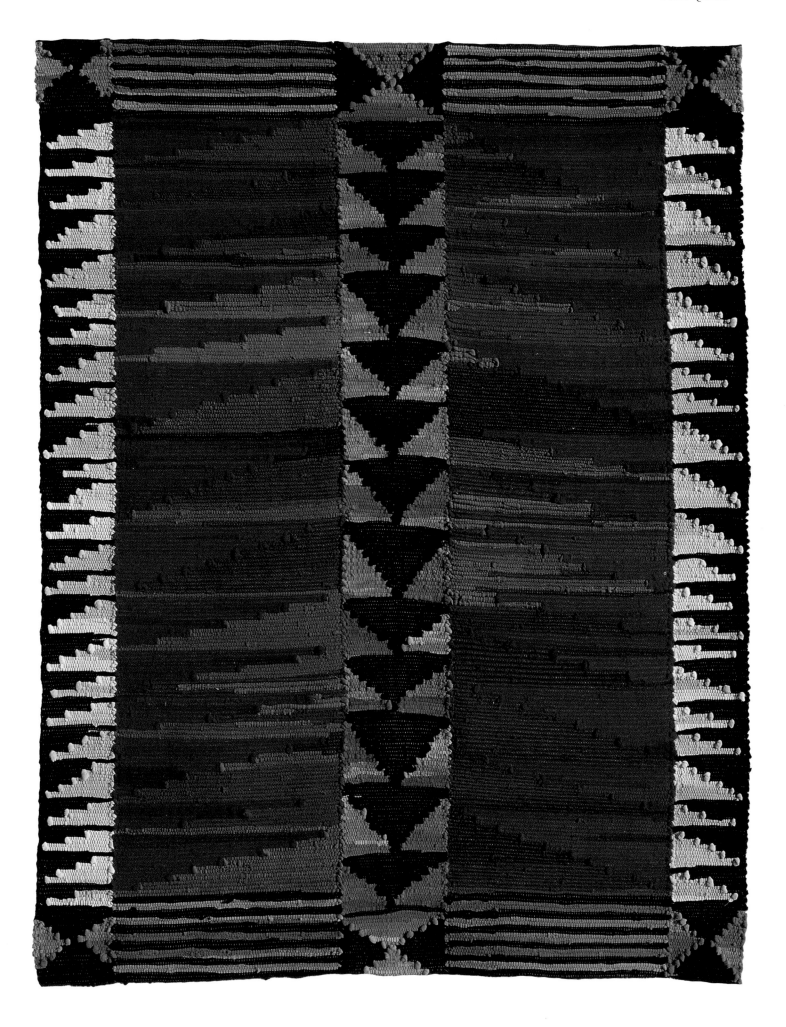

# BEAR'S PAW

The concept that quilts might be viable as an art form did not jell with me until late 1976 after I finished PETER'S QUILT (page 58). But the seed of that idea was planted in 1973 when I was exposed to an unusual quilt . . . a quilt that had been made for a baby. I was living in Cambridge, Ohio, at the time and was attending the quilting bees at the Senior Citizen Center so I could learn to hand quilt. It was there that I met Berenice Dunlap who invited me to her home to see a quilt she kept in her cedar chest. I remember her saying that the wool fabrics in the quilt came from shirts worn by her grandfather. But I was not prepared for how the wools had been transformed into a visual masterpiece. Out of the cedar chest came the most stunning quilt I had ever seen! My heart pounded! It was in perfect condition having never been used since it was finished in 1905. I was overwhelmed. Only three colors had been used . . . black, red and green. I loved the color combination. But all that black? So much black! How could Sarah Dunn have been so daring to use so much black? Especially when the quilt was intended for a baby? For Berenice, in fact.

Some might find the black overbearing, but to my eye the black enjoyed an absolutely dynamic relationship with the red and the green. "Dynamic" described the spirit pervading this quilt not overbearing. Sarah Dunn was willing to say through this quilt to her granddaughter that: "I am a strong person. I have ideas. I am not afraid. I can make strong statements. I was here. Know me. I value you. Don't forget me."

I have never forgotten that quilt. Was it fate that I saw it? In three more years it would act as a catalyst, pushing me toward quiltmaking as an art form to which I wanted to devote my life.

❖ *(Below)*
*NATHANIEL'S*
*QUILT, 1973-74,*
*(87" x 100").*

In 1973, I pored through one of my favorite books, *The Romance of the Patchwork Quilt in America* by Hall and Kretsinger, and chose two blocks, "Crazy Ann" and "Star-of-Hope" and combined them with a striking border. I shopped for the fabrics and then commissioned Berenice Dunlap to hand piece and hand quilt the top. I wanted this quilt for my four-year-old son, Nathaniel. I never thought of

❖ (Left) KING'S X,
©Nancy Crow,
1974-75,
(72" x 90"),
©Nancy Crow,
cotton and blends.
Collection of
Wayne Lawson,
Director of the
Ohio Arts Council.

❖ (Below)
WHIRLIGIG,
©Nancy Crow,
1975, (72" x 92"),
Cotton and blends.
Collection of the
artist.

Photographs of
KING'S X and
WHIRLIGIG
by Nancy Crow.

making it myself. I was too busy weaving, and Berenice was "the quiltmaker," not I.

In the KING'S X above (1974-75), I thought I was being wildly experimental because I chose more than the usual two or three colors, and I used all solids. I used not only one brown . . . but four different shades of brown plus black and white. I remember feeling very smug, very original! I thought the colors fit the strength of the pattern. I worked on this quilt for a year because I hand pieced it. And I never hand pieced a quilt again! I cannot remember who hand quilted it.

The WHIRLIGIG quilt at right (1975) represents my departure into the bright colors I used in my weaving. I was elated about finding just the right striped fabric to help create the sense of whirling. This is the only quilt I ever helped to hand quilt . . . my stitches were even but not small! I have used this quilt on my bed for the past 10 years, and it clashes with everything in my bedroom!

# QUILTS: (1976)

During 1976 I made:
PETER'S QUILT
CROSSES

❖ *(Above) PETER'S QUILT, ©Nancy Crow, 1976, (74" x 74"), hand quilted by Velma Brill. Collection of Mary Crow. Photograph by Nancy Crow.*

Although I based PETER'S QUILT on log cabin patterning, I thought I did something unusual with the background. I did have a template for each shape as I knew nothing of strip-piecing. I marked

the quilting lines very close as I liked that effect.

CROSSES is the only other quilt I made in 1976 . . . only two quilts. I was fascinated by log cabin patterns and kept

trying to do "something original" with them. I used color gradations in this quilt that became the forerunner of my INTERLACINGS quilts. For the border, I used my own interpretation of "Roman Stripe." This was my first "huge" quilt, and I laid it out on my studio floor and stood on the table to see how it looked. I had templates for all the parts. There is no strip-piecing in it.

❖ *(Above)*
*CROSSES,*
*©Nancy Crow,*
*1976, (96" x 96"),*
*handquilted by a*
*group of Ohio*
*Holmes County*
*Amish women.*
*Collection of the*
*artist.*

# QUILTS: (1977)

STUDIO: ATHENS, OHIO

During 1977 I made six quilts:
DIMINUTION
INCARNATION
CRUCIFIXION
RESURRECTION
4 PAPAVER AGAINST AN AZURE SKY
BRILL

Three of the quilts, DIMINUTION, 4 PAPAVER and BRILL, were totally unrelated to one another or to anything else while three of the quilts became my "first series." This is very important because as I became more absorbed by quilt making I began to work in series more often. By 1985 all my quilts were parts of series. After 1985, in fact, I found it exciting and far more efficient to work on three different series at once.

I began work on DIMINUTION the beginning of 1977 by continuing with the 96" x 96" size I had established for CROSSES. I was intrigued by that size . . . 96" x 96." I found I liked working with bigger and bigger blocks. Since I was working with detailed drawings with all the shapes and colors worked out, I simply made the templates and cut out the fabrics. I laid all the pieces out on the floor of my attic studio (Athens, Ohio). My floor was too small so I remember parts of the quilt top would disappear underneath my work table. Nonetheless, I had to get up onto my work table, stand-up and stare down in order to see the whole quilt. Sometimes I even put a step ladder on top of the table to get even further away visually. It was all quite awkward and frustrating and . . . thrilling. I think I "thought I invented the monster-size contemporary quilt!" Of course, I ended up walking all over the pieces lying on the floor until I got them sewn together.

Meantime I was working on my tapestry weaving down on the first floor where I had several looms set up in the living room and foyer.

When I began the three religious quilts, I drew out my ideas and included colors that had symbolic meaning. Red for blood, yellow for betrayal, purple for passion, blue for people, green for hope, white for good and black for evil. The border for each of these quilts was borrowed from CROSSES. Except that now the border would represent the struggle between good and evil (white and black). The amounts of each are different in each of these quilts. Christ is represented in the center of each quilt and the two thieves are on either side. Again I had made templates for all parts of these quilts. I used strip-piecing only once out of absolute necessity. I needed to make thorns to go around the crosses in the CRUCIFIXION quilt so I strip-pieced very narrow pieces of fabric. It never occurred to me that most of the quilt could have been made with strip-piecing! In fact the word "strip-piecing" was not in my vocabulary yet.

In the RESURRECTION quilt I wanted to portray the sense of flooding sunlight and, of course, good (white) winning out over evil (black). Notice the border. The hand quilting is especially superb in this quilt.

❖ *(Above)*
*DIMINUTION,*
*©Nancy Crow,*
*1977,*
*(96" x 96"), hand*
*quilted by group of*
*Amish women,*
*Holmes County,*
*Ohio. Collection of*
*Irena and Algis*
*Mickunas.*

❖ (Above)
INCARNATION,
© Nancy Crow,
1977, (96" x 96"),
hand quilted by a
group of Ohio
Amish women,
Holmes County.

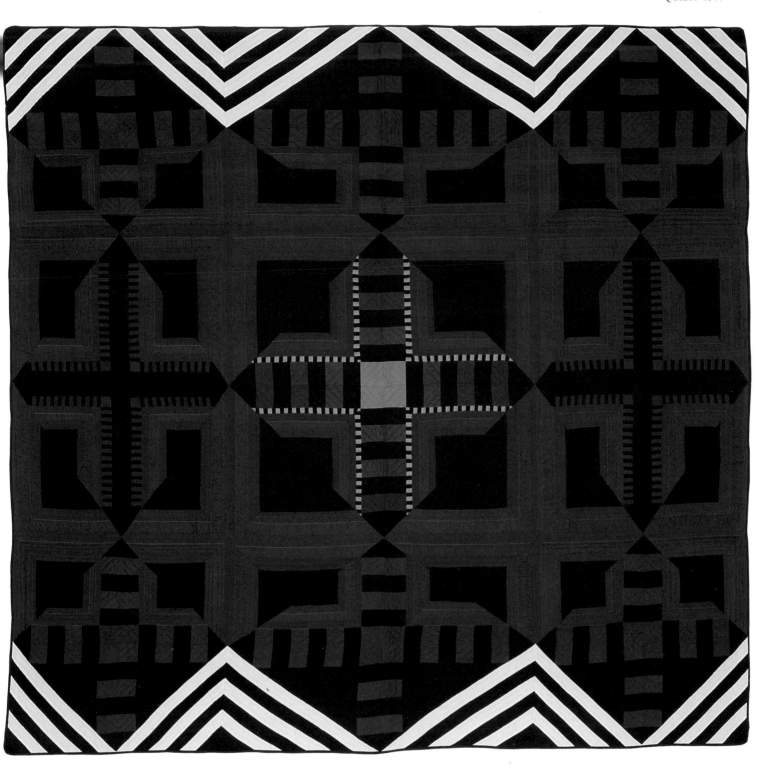

❖ *(Above)*
*CRUCIFIXION,*
*©Nancy Crow,*
*1977, (96" x 96"),*
*hand quilted by a*
*group of Ohio*
*Amish women,*
*Holmes County.*

❖ *(Above) RESUR-*
*RECTION, ©Nancy*
*Crow, 1977,*
*(96" x 96"),*
*hand quilted.*
*Private collection.*
*Photograph by*
*Nancy Crow.*

# THE FULL USE OF STRIP-PIECING.

When I began thinking about making this quilt, I had come to realize that "strip-piecing" was a viable technique, and that it could be used anywhere in a quilt! I was incredibly excited! I strip-pieced every part of 4 PAPAVER except the border which I marked to mimic poppy leaves and buds. This quilt is based on my experimentation with oriental poppies which I grew from seed and then photographed at every stage.

❖ *(Above) The underside of an oriental poppy (Papaver). 1977. Photograph by Nancy Crow.*

❖ *(Left) 4 PAPAVER AGAINST AN AZURE SKY, ©Nancy Crow, 1977, (76" x 76"), hand quilted by Velma Brill. Collection of The Massillon Museum of Fine Arts, Massillon, Ohio. Photograph by Nancy Crow.*

# BRILL

I do not know why I made BRILL. It is so different from everything else. At the time I think I wanted to work with curvilinear shapes and did not know how to piece them so I tried reverse applique. By the end of 1978 and the beginning of 1979, I was using many curved shapes in my quilts and piecing them directly.

I named this quilt in honor of Velma Brill for all the hand quilting she had done for me. Velma was always absolutely dependable.

❖ *(Opposite page) BRILL, ©Nancy Crow, 1977, (72" x 96"), hand quilted by Velma Brill. Collection of Maisie Peterson. Photograph by Nancy Crow.*

# QUILTS: (1978)

STUDIO: ATHENS, OHIO

During 1978 I made 8 quilts:
MATISSE PLAIN
MATISSE WITH WHITE
MATISSE WITH BLACK
GAILLARDIAS
NO BLACK, PLEASE!
WHAT A RELIEF!
BLUE AND BLACK STUDY I
BLUE AND BLACK STUDY II

Starting in 1978, I began to strip-piece as much of each new quilt as possible. I was in love with the technique. It was freeing and fascinating! The possibilities were endless. Each new refinement of a strip-piecing technique lead to new understanding. I soon realized it would take a lifetime to learn to use it effectively and sensitively.

I began 1978 with the MATISSE series. I wanted to experiment with pastels. So I decided to make three quilts. The first one would be plain. It would have only pastel colors. But the second would have a white grid riding over the surface and the third would have a black grid. I wanted to see how the pastels were effected by first the white and then the black.

I strip-pieced light and dark values together in many, many different combinations before starting MATISSE PLAIN. In fact, I had so much fabric left over that I used it in both of the other two quilts.

Velma Brill hand quilted all three quilts in succession but sent a letter of complaint back with MATISSE WITH BLACK saying she would not quilt anymore quilts with black fabric in them. Black was too hard on her eyes.

Although I sympathized, I was devastated! I have never wanted any outside limitations on my color usage.

Meantime I started GAILLARDIAS. I used the same idea of diagonal strips as I had used in the MATISSE quilts. But this time I completely changed the colors. I tried to imitate the colors of the Gaillardias growing in my garden. I wanted to achieve the sense of their spirit. So many of the Gaillardias had strong varied patterning. I developed this quilt on the wall! Oh, yes, my studio wall! After hearing my increasingly strident complaints about having to lay out my quilts on the floor, my husband, John, bought two 4' x 8' white celotex boards at the lumber yard and trucked them home. He nailed them into the studs of my attic studio instantly creating an 8' x 8' working wall. I could push pins into the celotex so easily because it was made of pressed paper. I was elated! My life changed forever! Everything became so much easier. I could see what I was doing. Such a simple but important thing: to see what you are doing easily.

Knowing that I really could not use dark colors or black for the next quilt since Velma would be quilting it, I began with salmon and added purple. Ugh! It became uglier and uglier and began pushing me around. I didn't have the slightest idea of what I was doing, but I kept going until I finished. When I shipped the top off to Velma, I named it NO BLACK, PLEASE!

The next quilt was a joy to make because I could use black. Mrs. Levi Mast would be quilting it. I was so hungry for joyful colors that I made this quilt rapidly. I called it WHAT A RELIEF! It was the first quilt in which I pieced curves by machine.

❖ *(Above)*
*MATISSE PLAIN,*
*©Nancy Crow,*
*1978,(64" x 64"),*
*hand quilted by*
*Velma Brill.*
*Collection of Anne*
*and Peter Gilleran,*
*Michigan.*
*Photograph by*
*Nancy Crow.*

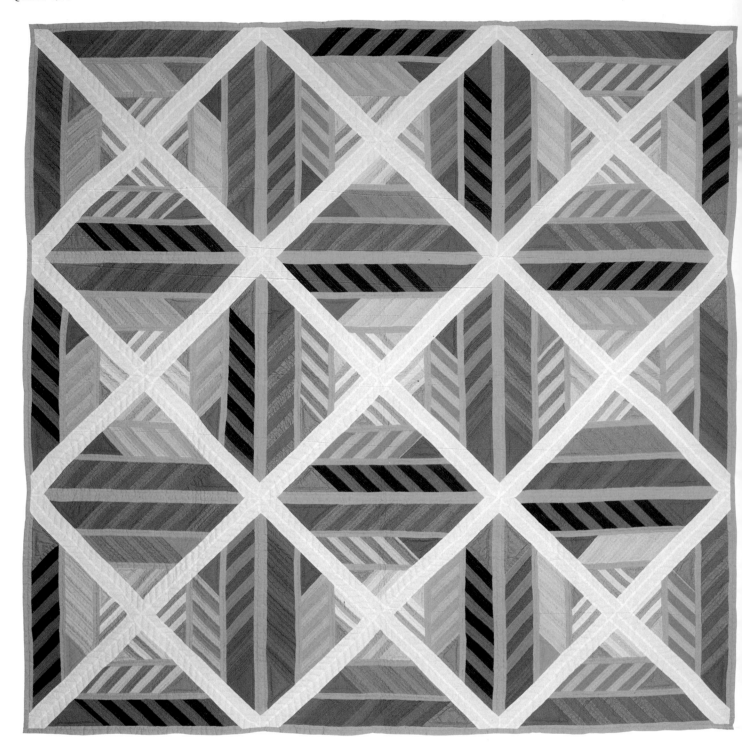

❖ *(Above)*
*MATISSE WITH*
*WHITE, ©Nancy*
*Crow, 1978,*
*(84" x 84"),*
*hand quilted by*
*Velma Brill.*

❖ *(Above)*
*MATISSE WITH*
*BLACK, ©Nancy*
*Crow, 1978,*
*(72" x 72"),*
*hand quilted by*
*Velma Brill.*
*Collection of June*
*and Robert Roffler,*
*Idaho. Photograph*
*by Nancy Crow.*

❖ (Right)
GAILLARDIAS,
©Nancy Crow,
1978, (72" x 72"),
hand quilted by
Velma Brill.
Collection of
Marjorie Addison,
Ohio. Photograph
by Nancy Crow.

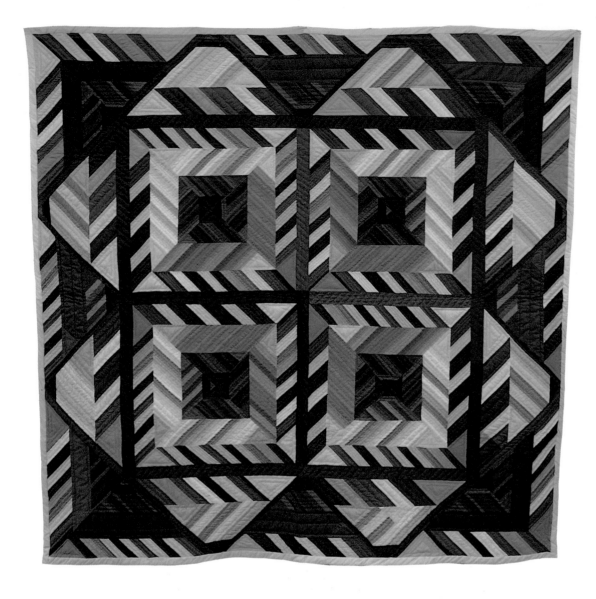

❖ (Right) NO
BLACK, PLEASE!,
©Nancy Crow,
1978, (78" x 78"),
hand quilted by
Velma Brill.
Photograph by
Nancy Crow.

❖ (Opposite page)
WHAT A RELIEF!,
©Nancy Crow,
1978, (48" x 48"),
hand quilted by
Mattie Raber.
Collection of
K-Mart
International
Headquarters,
Troy, Michigan.
Photograph by
Nancy Crow.

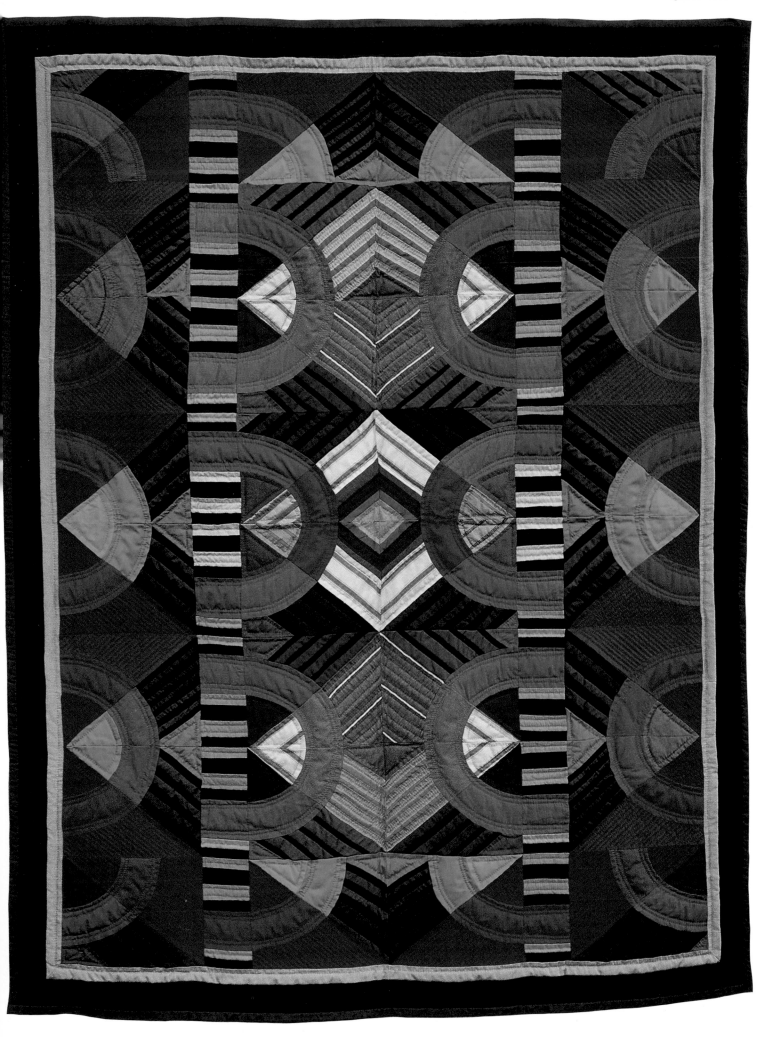

❖ (Above) BLUE
AND BLACK
STUDY I, ©Nancy
Crow, 1978,
(60" x 60"),
hand quilted by
group of Ohio
Amish women.

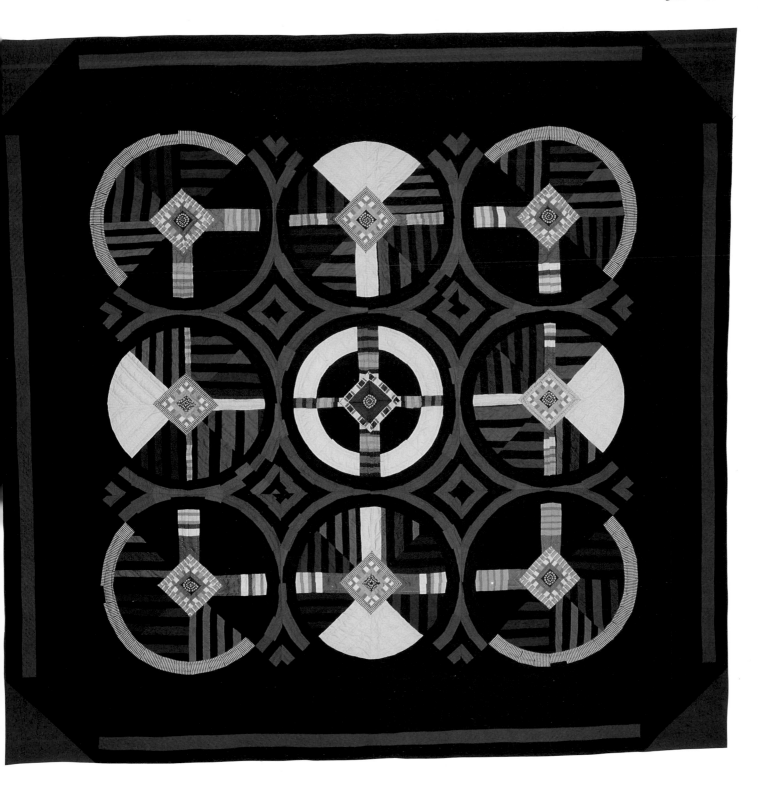

❖ *(Above) BLUE AND BLACK STUDY II, ©Nancy Crow, 1978, (80" x 80"), hand quilted by Mrs. Abe Yoder, Holmes County, Ohio.*

# QUILTS: (1979)

STUDIO: ATHENS,OHIO,
UNTIL AUGUST 1979.

During 1979 I made a total commitment to contemporary quiltmaking. I put away my looms and set a goal of at least 20 quilts for 1979. I have not included all of those 20 quilts here because some of them were not recorded at all and some were awful. I have included those quilts I felt were significant:

CROSSES AND SPRING (January)
JANUARY I (second week of Jan.)
JANUARY II (third week of Jan.)
JULY STUDY (fourth week of Jan.)
FEBRUARY I (first week of Feb.)
FEBRUARY II (second week of Feb.)
MARCH STUDY
ATHEN'S FAREWELL
RACHEL'S QUILT
LOG CABIN FOR MOTHER

❖ *(Above)*
*JANUARY STUDY I,*
*©Nancy Crow,*
*1979, (65" x 65"),*
*hand quilted by*
*Lovina Yoder.*
*Collection of*
*Bonnie K. Miller,*
*Ohio.*
*Photograph by*
*Nancy Crow.*

JANUARY STUDY II was one of those very few quilts that was not a "struggle" for me. Even though I used an immense number of templates with lots of curved shapes and lots of different fabrics, I was able to sew this top in one week.

❖ *(Above)*
*JANUARY STUDY II,*
*©Nancy Crow,*
*1979, (80" x 80"),*
*hand quilted by*
*Velma Brill.*

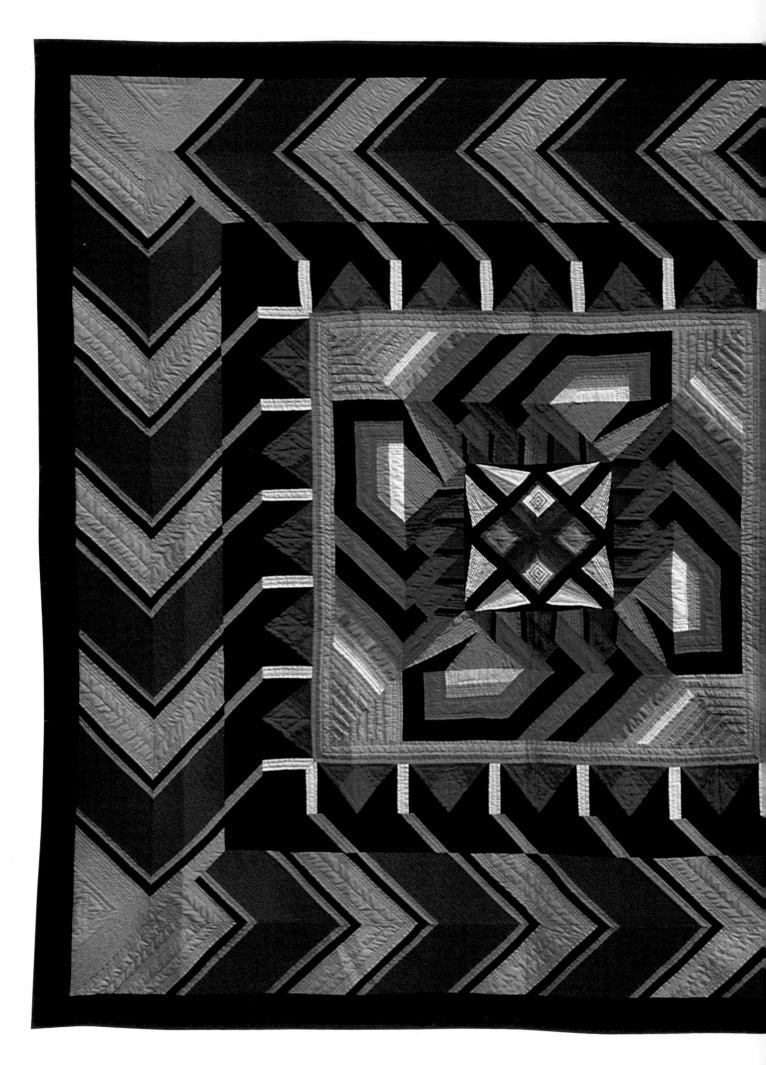

❖ *(Left)*
*JULY STUDY,*
*©Nancy Crow,*
*1978-79,*
*(80" x 80"),*
*hand quilted by*
*Mrs. Levi Mast.*
*Collection of*
*Doreen and*
*Fred Pallini, Ohio.*
*Photograph by*
*Nancy Crow.*

I actually started JULY STUDY in July of 1978 but I did not finish it until the fourth week of January 1979. I began in the very middle and simply kept adding on bands of designs until I felt the quilt was the size I wanted and that looked right. The hand quilting is wonderful in this quilt. I marked the lines very close.

❖ *(Below) Detail*
*of JULY STUDY,*
*©Nancy Crow,*
*1978-79.*
*Photograph by*
*Nancy Crow.*

❖ *(Above)*
*FEBRUARY STUDY I,*
*©Nancy Crow,*
*1979, (48" x 48"),*
*hand quilted*
*by Velma Brill.*
*Collection of*
*Frank Ching.*
*Photograph*
*by  Nancy Crow.*

❖ *(Above)*
*FEBRUARY STUDY II,*
*©Nancy Crow, 1979,*
*(60" x 60"), hand*
*quilted by Velma Brill.*

❖ *(Far right)*
*MARCH STUDY*
*hanging in the*
*window of the*
*American Craft*
*Museum in New*
*York City. 1980.*
*Photograph by*
*Nancy Crow.*

I consider MARCH STUDY my "lucky quilt" because it brought a lot of attention to my career. Not only was it included in the 1980 exhibition at the American Craft Museum, but a detail of it appeared on the cover of the April/May 1980 issue of *American Craft Magazine.* All of a sudden I began to receive invitations to exhibit my work.

❖ *(Right)*
*MARCH STUDY*
*in-progress on the*
*wall of my attic*
*studio in Athens,*
*Ohio. 1979.*
*Photograph by*
*Nancy Crow.*

❖ *(Above)*
*MARCH STUDY,*
*©Nancy Crow,*
*1979, (80" x 80"),*
*hand quilted by*
*Mrs. Levi Mast.*

❖ *(Opposite page)*
*ATHENS FAREWELL,*
*©Nancy Crow,*
*1979, (48" x 52"),*
*hand quilted by*
*Velma Brill.*
*Collection of*
*General Foods*
*Corporation.*
*Photograph by*
*Nancy Crow.*

❖ *(Below)*
*Detail of ATHENS*
*FAREWELL,*
*©Nancy Crow,*
*Photograph by*
*Nancy Crow.*

I used a combination of square and rectangular blocks to make ATHENS FAREWELL, my "emotional good-bye" to Athens, Ohio, and my home of five years.

I remember feeling quite "experimental" in my use of prints. And I remember thinking my color combinations very unusual . . . lots of rust. But I never could resolve the center. It looks like a football or an eye. I never wanted to part with this quilt as I felt it was the "beginning" of a whole series. Perhaps I will go back and explore it further. Meantime I did use blocks from it for my LADY OF GUADALUPE II, 1987.

❖ *(Above)*
*RACHEL'S QUILT,*
*©Nancy Crow,*
*1979, (74" x 74"),*
*hand quilted by*
*Velma Brill.*
*Collection of*
*Rhoda and*
*Murray Levinsohn,*
*Ohio. Photograph*
*by Nancy Crow.*

I made this quilt for my mother to use on her bed.

❖ (Above)
*LOG CABIN
FOR MOTHER,
©Nancy Crow,
(78" x 78"),
hand quilted by
Mrs. Levi Mast.*

# MOVING TO THE FARM
## (Fall 1979)

August 1979 marked the final move away from Athens, Ohio, and five of the fullest years of my life. There I had met the women who I would come to love dearly. We became catalysts for one another, pushing and pulling each other to grow. And we grew fast because the "time was right." We wanted to make quilts. And we wanted to become better and better as quickly as possible.

A small group of us women had managed to mount the first Quilt National at The Dairy Barn. Again the "time was right" and the enthusiasm high. We started with no money, but we were determined. When we acquired the barn (it was the only building large enough in Athens to hold an extensive exhibit of quilts) from the state of Ohio for $1.00, it had not been used for several years. It was filthy. Filled with cow manure, thick with cobwebs, broken windows, pigeons flying in and

out and milking stanchions in place. Our first money-making project . . . was scooping up the dried manure, bagging it and selling it for fertilizer. It may sound funny, but it took months of time by volunteers just to complete all of the shoveling. Afterwards a power wash company came in and sprayed down the walls and disinfected them. The milking stanchions stayed in place during that first Quilt National. There was no money to have them cut out. The biggest worry after the show opened was to keep viewers from tripping and falling into the shallow manure ditches (though absolutely clean!). It was a very, very heady experience to know that a group of women (most not quiltmakers) could work together so well, so unselfishly, with no pay to make Quilt National become a reality.

The move to our farm (45 miles northwest of Athens and 28 miles east of Columbus) marked the beginning of a new type of growth referred to as "coming to terms with oneself." My first response to the farm was, "Oh, how romantic!" That response reversed itself within days. I think I was truly horrified to find that the long lane in front of our house was accu-

rately symbolic. We were cut off from the world! I believed it! It was a long way down to the outside world, and the outside world felt intimidated about entering the long lane up to our house.

A normally gregarious person, I suddenly began talking to myself a lot. I made phone calls out, but they were all long-distance and after awhile we could not afford them. So phone calling dwindled to letter writing which in time dwindled also. For the first time in my 36 years, I began to suffer a "profound depression." I could not work. I had no interest in quilts anymore. I cried most of the time. I stared out the windows down the lane hoping that someone would come visit. I needed to be reassured that "life would be all right." I knew I was on the verge of a complete nervous breakdown, and that I faced several choices: get divorced and leave . . . or shake off the depression.

The first choice was no option because I loved my husband and two sons. But how could I deal with the depression? Whenever I walked outside I felt a "renewal." So I took that as my clue, picked up my camera and began walking the farm, every part of it, day after day, looking, training my eye until I finally began "seeing." I became re-acquainted with the sky, with trees outlined against the sky, with the wind, with the wind blowing stands of weeds, with clouds. I photographed the lane at all times of the day, likewise the house, the fields, the trees, everything. I looked for composition, texture, line, color, life, spirit, and I finally found strength, inner strength. I discovered I was beginning to take responsibility for making myself happy. I was finally willing to accept that this was how it was going to be. I could not run across the street to find stimulation with friends. There would be no theaters or museums in walking distance. Instead, what replaced all of this and what ultimately became more interesting to me were the internal dialogues that developed as I became more passionate about my quilt making, as I read and read from a growing library of art books, as I accepted nature, its beauty, its terror and its comfort.

# BUILDING
# A STUDIO
## (1980-1984)

*All photographs on
these two pages
were taken by
Nancy Crow.*

In early 1980, "building a studio" became one of my focuses. I wanted a decent studio, a professional studio. Since graduate school I had always used a bedroom wherever we lived. Now I wanted a studio separate from the house. I needed psychological distancing without having to drive somewhere to a rented space.

I had just received a $10,000.00 grant from the National Endowment for the Arts and had saved $6,000.00 from doing custom leather work. I was ready to build! But $16,000.00 does not build a studio! Renovation of an existing barn seemed the answer. My carpenter, Michael Shreyer, told me a 25' x 30' granary could be moved intact up to just behind the house so I could walk out my kitchen door across 20 ft. to my studio door. It would take $4,000.00 to have the studio moved (it took two weeks) and then the

renovating could begin. Since my money kept running out even with a loan, the complete renovation took four years. Finally the studio was finished with an added upstairs office and a full basement giving me 1,600 square feet. After I moved into my beautiful new space, I quickly outgrew it, and so I hired Mike to build a 20' x 20' addition (1986-87). I needed proper storage space for already finished quilts, a wall on which to photograph them, a bathroom and more shelves for fabrics and my bulging library. I also wanted a place to sit, read and daydream, away from the constant stimulation of quilts in progress on the walls of my main studio.

Note: All floors, woodwork, doors and shelving are made of yellow pine. The original beams are beech and have been left exposed. The office is on the second floor of the main studio.

❖ *(Opposite page at very top) My old studio in 14' x 14' front parlor of the house.*

❖ *(Left to right) The 25' x 30' granary before it was picked up and moved.*

  *The granary barn moved up to behind house and renovated.*

  *House (originally) with shed behind.*

  *House after granary barn was moved in place.*

  *Inside of granary barn showing floor beams and corn bins just before the building was moved.*

  *Same view after renovation.*

❖ *(Left, this page) Back of house and studio with new addition.*

❖ *(Below, left & right) Two views inside the new addition showing the incredible carpentry skill of Mike Shreyer, Baltimore, Ohio.*

# 20' x 20'
# ADDITION
## (1986-1987)

# QUILTS: (1980-1982)

## NEWE SERIES (1980)

Quilts began to flow out of me once again. I chose the name "NEWE" for the first series of four quilts that mark my recovery from not being able to make quilts for four months. I used the same block in all four quilts but added and subtracted shapes depending on how I felt. I experimented with lots of strip-piecing in this series, especially with the concept of using strip-piecing to form "new shapes."

Immediately after finishing these quilts, the BITTERSWEET Series poured out, one after the other until I had made 22 quilts in all. They document the bittersweet relationship between two people who love one another, and the final growth into independence and acceptance of responsibility for one's own happiness.

❖ *(Below) NEWE I in progress, 1980. Photograph by Nancy Crow. (In old 14' x 14' studio in house.)*

❖ *(Below) NEWE I,*
*©Nancy Crow,*
*1980, (80" x 80").*
*Collection of*
*Nancy Dickenson,*
*Ohio. Photograph*
*by Nancy Crow.*

❖ (Below)
NEWE II, ©Nancy
Crow, 1980,
(68½" x 68½"),
hand quilted by
Mrs. Levi Mast.

❖ *(Left) Interior of my studio in the 14' x 14' front parlor of our house. I often went outside onto the front porch and looked through the window to get enough distance from the quilt I was working on. Part of my basket collection is lined up on the walls behind me. I worked in this studio from 1980-1984. Photograph by Jean Alexander Greenwald. 1982.*

❖ *(Left) Interior of my new 25' x 30' studio, the 120 year old granary was renovated over the period 1980-1984. I designed the large red oak work tables and had three of them made by Ohio Amish. They are extra high to help prevent back problems. INTERLACINGS I hangs on the wall in the background. Photograph by Jean Alexander Greenwald. 1983.*

❖ *(Above)*
*NEWE III,*
*©Nancy Crow,*
*1980, (56" x 56"),*
*hand quilted by*
*Mrs. Albert*
*Swartzentruber.*

❖ *(Above)*
*NEWE IV,*
*©Nancy Crow,*
*1980, (56" x 56"),*
*hand quilted by*
*Mrs. Eli Troyer.*

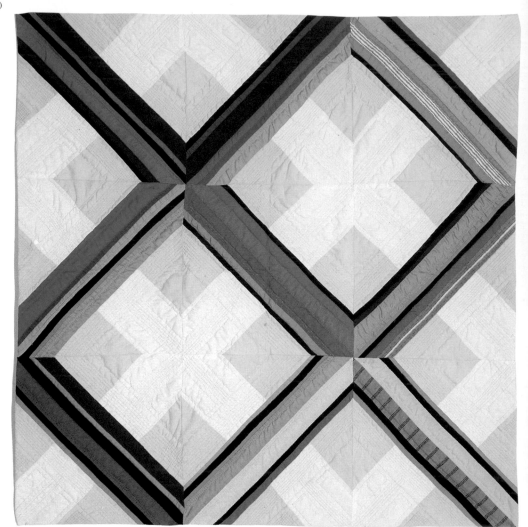

## Series: BITTERSWEET (1980-1982)

The first 11 BITTERSWEET quilts were all small, based on a nine-block repeat of a 12" block. Within the block, I made up nearly 50 different templates which gave me lots to experiment with. However, in the first three quilts I began with just a few shapes as the block itself symbolizes me . . . and I want to show how one changes, perhaps getting more complex.

❖ *(Above)*
*BITTERSWEET I,*
*©Nancy Crow,*
*1980, (36" x 36"),*
*hand quilted by*
*Velma Brill.*

❖ *(Right)*
*BITTERSWEET II,*
*©Nancy Crow,*
*1980, (36" x 36"),*
*hand quilted by*
*Velma Brill.*

❖ *(Left)*
*BITTERSWEET III,*
*©Nancy Crow,*
*1980, (39" x 39"),*
*hand quilted by*
*Mrs. Levi Mast.*

The first four BITTERSWEET quilts are about the relationship between two people. With BITTERSWEET V, the relationship is broken. Things b e c o m e " s u r f a c e y " (surface deep) again. Everything seems meaningless as depression sets in . . . with BITTERSWEETS VI, VII and VIII.

❖ *(Bottom left)*
*BITTERSWEET IV,*
*©Nancy Crow,*
*1980, (38" x 38"),*
*hand quilted by*
*Rose Augenstein.*

❖ *(Right)*
*BITTERSWEET V,*
*©Nancy Crow,*
*1980, (39" x 39").*
*Photograph by*
*Nancy Crow.*

BITTERSWEET
V is the transitional
quilt into the
period of depres-
sion portrayed in
BITTERSWEET VI,
VII and VIII. In
making this quilt,
I went back and
used the same
templates as I had
used in BITTER-
SWEET I.

❖ *(Bottom right)*
*BITTERSWEET VI,*
*©Nancy Crow,*
*1980, (38" x 38"),*
*hand quilted by*
*Rose Augenstein.*

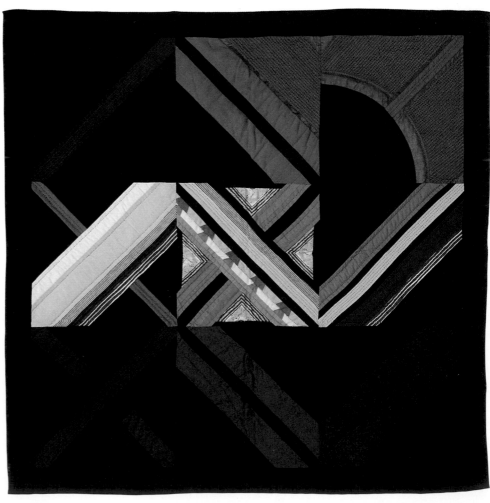

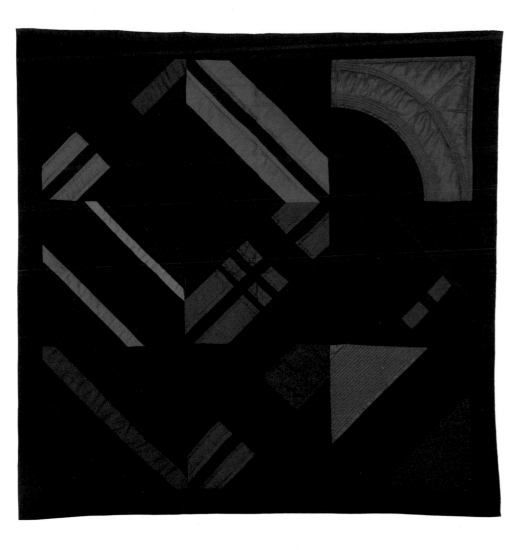

❖ *(Top left)*
*BITTERSWEET VII,*
*©Nancy Crow,*
*1980, (38" x 38"),*
*hand quilted by*
*Rose Augenstein.*

In all three of the depression quilts, I used only a few templates and with each quilt less color. I wanted to show that the world of a depressed person is colorless and monotonous. Technically I wanted lines of extremely close hand quilting set against broad areas with no handquilting.

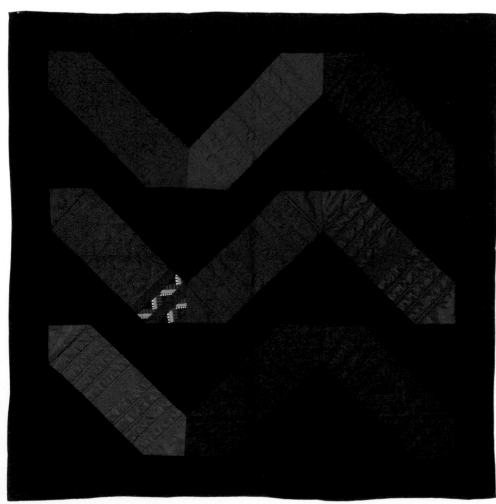

❖ *(Bottom left)*
*BITTERSWEET VIII,*
*©Nancy Crow,*
*1980, (38" x 38"),*
*hand quilted by*
*Rose Augenstein. I*
*subtitled number*
*eight, "Depression*
*is getting boring!"*

❖ *(Top right)*
*BITTERSWEET IX,*
*©Nancy Crow,*
*1980, (39" x 39").*
*Photograph by*
*Nancy Crow.*

In BITTER-SWEET IX, I used the same templates as I used in BITTERSWEETS I and V. It is the strip-piecing that makes it look so complex. This is the transitional quilt into my becoming independent. With BITTERSWEET X, I begin to grow as a person in my own right, and with XI the transformation is profound. That is why the quilt is so different from the first ten. I chose to end the first part of the BITTERSWEET Series with an uneven number, as uneven numbers are more exciting to me.

❖ *(Bottom right)*
*BITTERSWEET XI,*
*©Nancy Crow,*
*1980, (36" x 36"),*
*hand quilted by*
*Velma Brill.*

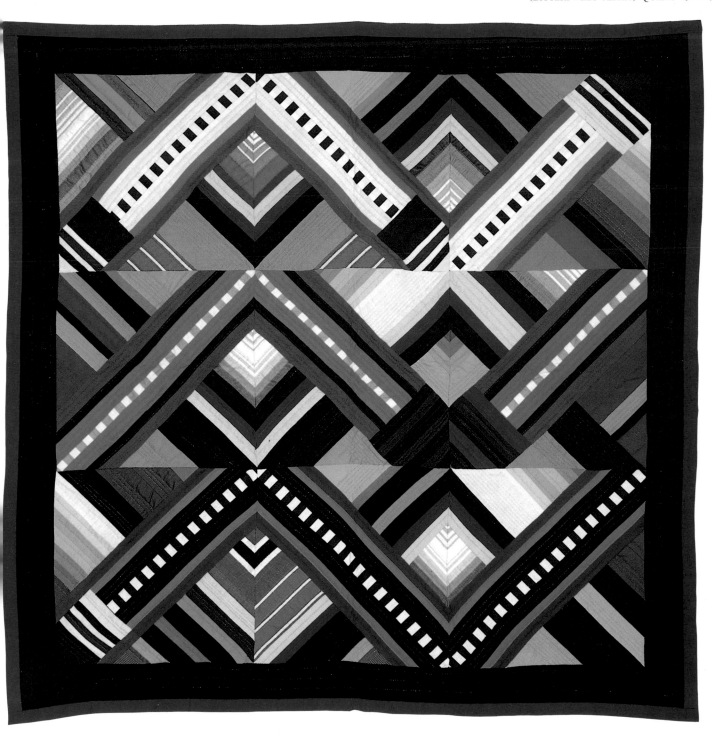

❖ *(Above)*
*BITTERSWEET X,*
*©Nancy Crow,*
*1980,(40" x 40"),*
*hand quilted by*
*Rose Augenstein.*

❖ *(Above)*
*BITTERSWEET XII,*
*©Nancy Crow,*
*1980-81, (81" x 81"),*
*hand quilted by*
*Velma Brill.*
*Collection of the*
*Museum of American*
*Folk Art,*
*New York City.*
*Photograph by*
*Nancy Crow.*

All of the BITTERSWEET quilts came rapidly, in a rush. I learned so much from doing the first 11 that I am not sure I could have done the next 11 without having done those first. The impetus of energy was overwhelming.

Starting with BITTWERSWEET XII, I began using blocks that were 24" square but with the same break-up space as I used in the 12" blocks for the first 11 quilts.

❖ *(Above) BITTER-SWEET XIII, ©Nancy Crow, 1981, (95" x 95"), hand quilted by Velma Brill. Collection of The Vantage Companies, Atlanta, Georgia. Photograph by Nancy Crow.*

❖ *(Above)*
*BITTERSWEET XIV,*
*©Nancy Crow,*
*1981, (68½" x 68½"),*
*hand quilted by*
*Rose Augenstein.*
*Collection of*
*The American Craft*
*Museum,*
*New York City.*
*Photograph by*
*Nancy Crow.*

❖ *(Above)*
*BITTERSWEET XV,*
*©Nancy Crow,*
*1981, (82" x 82"),*
*hand quilted by*
*Mrs. Eli Troyer.*
*Collection of Jack*
*Lenor Larsen, New*
*York City.*
*Photograph by*
*Nancy Crow.*

❖ *(Above)*
*BITTERSWEET XVI,*
*©Nancy Crow, 1981,*
*(68½" x 68½"),*
*hand quilted by*
*Velma Brill.*

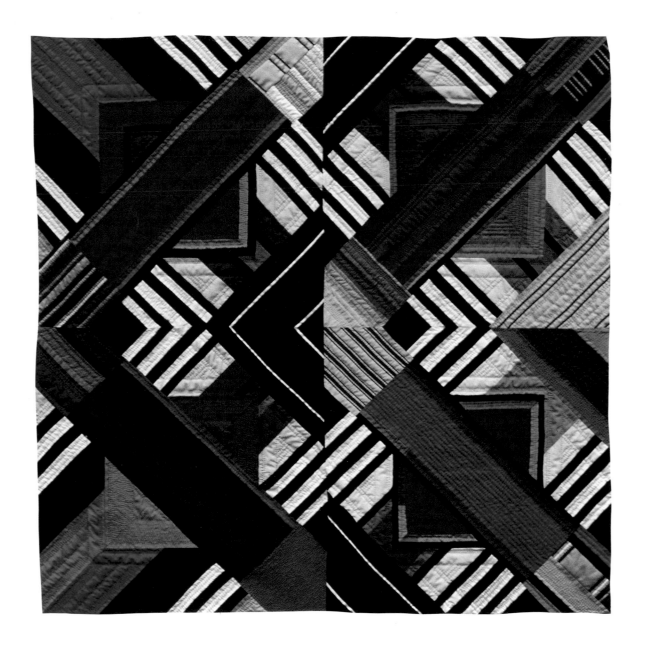

❖ *(Above) BIT-*
*TERSWEET XVII,*
*©Nancy Crow,*
*1981, (60" x 60"),*
*hand quilted by*
*Mrs. Levi Mast.*
*Collection of Anne*
*Heideman and*
*Peter Gilleran,*
*Brooklyn.*
*Photograph by*
*Nancy Crow.*

❖ *(Above)*
*BITTERSWEET XVIII,*
*©Nancy Crow,1981,*
*(60" x 60"), hand*
*quilted by Rose*
*Augenstein.*

❖ *(Above)*
*BITTERSWEET XIX,*
*©Nancy Crow,*
*1982, (60" x 60"),*
*hand quilted by*
*Rose Augenstein.*

❖ *(Above)*
*BITTERSWEET XX,*
*©Nancy Crow,*
*1982,*
*(68½" x 68½"),*
*hand quilted by*
*Velma Brill.*
*Collection of*
*Ashland Chemical*
*Corporation,*
*Columbus, Ohio.*
*Photograph by*
*Nancy Crow.*

❖ *(Above)*
*BITTERSWEET XXI,*
*©Nancy Crow,*
*1982, (77" x 77"),*
*hand quilted by*
*Rose Augenstein.*

❖ *(Above)*
*BITTERSWEET XXII,*
*©Nancy Crow,*
*1982, (60" x 60"),*
*hand quilted by*
*Mrs. Levi Mast.*
*Collection of*
*Mr. & Mrs. Joseph*
*Campochiaro,*
*California.*
*Photograph by*
*Nancy Crow.*

# MISCELLANEOUS QUILTS (1980-1982)

From 1980 to 1982, I made other miscellaneous quilts in and around the BITTERSWEET quilts. Work on the BITTERSWEET Series got too intense at times, and I had to back off and work on other quilts that did not have so much emotional content.

Up until I began the BITTERSWEET quilts, most of my series had consisted of no more than three to four quilts and those series were separated by many individual quilts that were not part of a series. Only with the start of the INTERLACINGS quilts in 1983 did I begin to work in series nearly all of the time. And the series began to stretch over periods of years. Now I can foresee that I might be spending 10-12 years or more working on and off on future series. I have begun a number of series in 1985, 1986 and 1987 that I am still interested in and want to continue with, namely LADY OF GUADALUPE, MEXICAN WHEELS, COLOR BLOCKS and DOUBLE MEXICAN WEDDING RINGS.

Back in 1980, I began the OCTOBER STUDY quilts thinking I would create my mother's flower garden with a wall around it. I made two versions side by side on my work wall using templates from the 12" block used in BITTERSWEET I. The actual title of both quilts is: FLOWERS AND FORMAL GARDEN BORDERS.

From these two quilts, I moved on to the NOVEMBER Series of three. In all three, I used the same 16" block with the intention of seeing how many different ways I could make the quilt simply by using all different types of strip-piecing and colors. Some strip-piecing was kept the same in all three quilts. I also wanted to play with illusions of depth. These quilts, like all of my quilts, were developed on the wall. They were not worked out ahead of time on paper, in detail, with color. I cannot work that way. I prefer to improvise on the wall using only pre-designed templates and blocks.

ANNUAL #1 was made in memory of my own flower garden that had turned out well one summer. I also wanted to work with green. Colors are a joy to me! I never have trouble with color, and it is the one unequivocal thing that gives true happiness to my life. I love putting colors together.

When I made JAPANESE STUDY, I had a great need for "simplicity," and so I used only a few colors against a great field of black. I unexpectedly produced a glowing effect. The format is based on a Japanese scroll.

I haven't the foggiest notion of why I made NEWE/BITT except that I wanted to play with the combination of a square block and a rectangle. I don't even know why I chose those colors!

I quickly went on to MARCH SKY and HIGH SPIRITS, quilts packed with emotions since they were based on my photographic studies of the sky over our farm. I used blocks from the BITTERSWEET Series to make these quilts.

CONTRADICTIONS is my interpretation of my love of flowers restrained by my need for symmetry while wanting to go beyond the boundaries. I had hoped this would be the start of a series but it never was . . . but I am still working on the idea behind it!

❖ *(Right)*
*OCTOBER STUDY I*
*and OCTOBER*
*STUDY II,*
*©Nancy Crow,*
*1980. Both are 60"*
*x 60". OCTOBER*
*STUDY I is in the*
*collection of David*
*Dickenson, II,*
*Cleveland.*
*OCTOBER STUDY*
*II is in the*
*collection of*
*Michael Gilleran,*
*Boston.*
*Photograph by*
*Nancy Crow.*

❖ *(Above)*
*NOVEMBER*
*STUDY I,*
*©Nancy Crow,*
*1980, (64" x 64"),*
*hand quilted by*
*Mrs. Levi Mast.*
*Collection of Lynn*
*Plotkin, St. Louis.*
*Photograph by*
*Nancy Crow.*

❖ *(Above)*
*NOVEMBER*
*STUDY II, 1980,*
*©Nancy Crow,*
*(64" x 64"),*
*hand quilted by*
*Velma Brill.*
*Collection of Lynn*
*Plotkin, St. Louis.*
*Photograph by*
*Nancy Crow.*

❖ *(Above)*
*NOVEMBER*
*STUDY III,*
*©Nancy Crow,*
*1980, (64" x 64"),*
*hand quilted by*
*Rose Augenstein.*

❖ *(Above)*
*ANNUAL #1,*
*©Nancy Crow, 1981,*
*65" x 65", hand*
*quilted by Mary and*
*Mattie Mast. This*
*quilt was included in*
*an exhibition titled:*
*"DESIGN IN AMERI-*
*CA" which toured*
*eastern Europe 1986-*
*1990. The exhibit*
*was sponsored by the*
*United States*
*Information Agency,*
*Washington, D.C.*

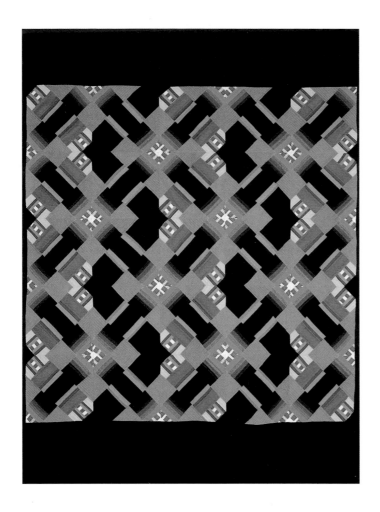

❖ *(Left)*
*JAPANESE STUDY,*
*©Nancy Crow,*
*1981, (64" x 84"),*
*hand quilted by*
*Mrs. Jacob*
*Hershberger.*

❖ *(Below)*
*NEWE/BITT,*
*©Nancy Crow,*
*1982, (54" x 54"),*
*hand quilted by*
*Velma Brill.*
*Private collection.*
*Photograph by*
*Nancy Crow.*

❖ *(Above left)*
*March sky*
*photographed by*
*Nancy Crow.*

❖ *(Above right)*
*MARCH SKY just*
*returned from the*
*quilter and ready*
*to be bound.*

❖ *(Right)*
*MARCH SKY,*
*©Nancy Crow,*
*1982, (48" x 48"),*
*hand quilted by*
*Rose Augenstein.*
*Private collection.*

Refer to pages IV and V to see the two photos of skies that influenced the making of this quilt. Pages VI and VII show this quilt in progress as a wider horizontal quilt before the size was reduced to a square of 48" x 48".

❖ *(Above)*
*HIGH SPIRITS,*
©*Nancy Crow,*
*1982, (65" x 65"),*
*hand quilted by*
*Mrs. Jacob*
*Hershberger.*

❖ *(Left)*
*HIGH SPIRITS in*
*progress in studio*
*inside our farm*
*home. 1982.*
*Photograph by*
*Nancy Crow.*

❖ *(Above)*
*CONTRADICTIONS,*
*©Nancy Crow,*
*1982, (91" x 91"),*
*hand quilted by*
*Rose Augenstein.*
*Photograph by*
*Nancy Crow.*

CONTRADICTIONS was chosen by Governor Richard F. Celeste and his wife, Dagmar, to be included in an exhibition called the "Governor's Residence Art Collection." This quilt was subsequently purchased and hung as a part of the permanent art collection in the Governor's mansion, Columbus, Ohio. Governor and Mrs. Celeste have been incredibly supportive of the arts in Ohio and have given strong support to the Ohio Arts Council,

considered to be one of the most widely-respected arts councils in the United States.

# Series: INTERLACINGS (1983-1986)

❖ (Below)
*INTERLACINGS I,*
*©Nancy Crow,*
*1983, (72" x 72").*
*Collection of*
*Roberta and*
*David Williamson.*
*Photograph by*
*Nancy Crow.*

The INTERLACINGS series grew out of my need to explore more fully the "cross shape" and gradations of colors by the use of strip-piecing. The border was borrowed from CROSSES done in 1976.

❖ *(Right) Original drawing for the INTERLACING series. Underneath is a 20" block-to-size with shapes drawn in. Both the block and the drawing are left on the wall for handy reference. 1983. Photograph by Nancy Crow.*

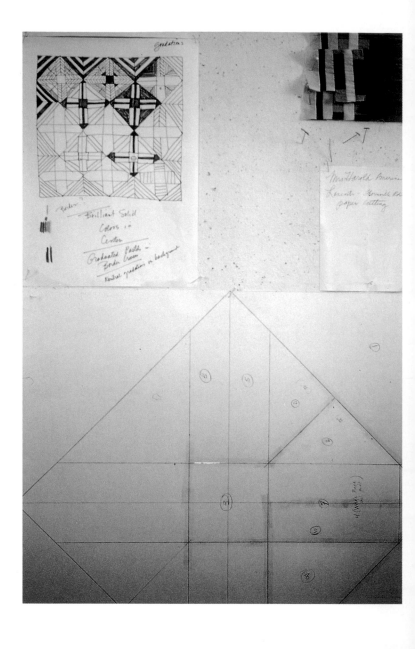

❖ *(Right) Laying in the outside border to determine the final size of INTERLACINGS II before developing the internal templates. Final size would be 60" x 60". 1983. Photograph by Nancy Crow.*

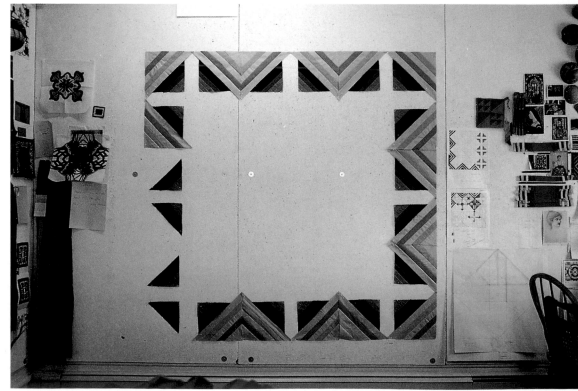

❖ *(Left) Strip-pieced gradations have been pinned into the cross shapes in the four corners of the quilt. Photograph by Nancy Crow. 1983.*

❖ *(Left) Much trial and error with strip-piecing of new fabrics goes on as the quilt is developed. Many strip-pieced fabrics are sewn, tried and not used after they have been cut out and pinned up on the wall because they do not work visually with everything else that is already there. One must not be afraid to waste fabric nor use a lot of time making these new "trial fabrics." Photograph by Nancy Crow. 1983.*

129

❖ *(Right)*
*INTERLACINGS II*
*in progress.*
*Photograph by*
*Nancy Crow.*
*1983.*

❖ *(Right ) Sewing*
*together one of the*
*long diagonals.*
*Photograph by*
*Nancy Crow.*
*1983.*

❖ (Left) Final
sewing together of
INTERLACINGS II,
part by part but in
diagonals.
Photograph by
Nancy Crow.

❖ (Left)
Interior of studio
showing position
of sewing table
and sewing
machine in
relationship to
work wall where
INTERLACINGS II
is pinned. This is
my second studio
in the front parlor
of the house before
I moved out to my
present studio in
the barn.
Photograph by
Nancy Crow.
1983.

❖ *(Above)*
*INTERLACINGS II,*
*©Nancy Crow,*
*1983, (60" x 60")*
*hand quilted by*
*Mrs. Levi Mast.*
*Collection of*
*Southwest General*
*Hospital, Berea,*
*Ohio. Photograph*
*by Nancy Crow.*

❖ *(Above)*
*INTERLACINGS III,*
*©Nancy Crow,*
*1985, (72" x 72"),*
*hand quilted by*
*Rose Augenstein.*

❖ (Above)
INTERLACINGS V,
©Nancy Crow,
1986, (72" x 72"),
hand quilted by
Rose Augenstein.
Photograph by
Nancy Crow.

❖ (Opposite page)
INTERLACINGS VI,
©Nancy Crow,
1986, (48" x 72"),
hand quilted by
Rose Augenstein.

❖ (Below)
*TRAMP ART I,*
*©Nancy Crow,*
*1983, (54" x 65"),*
*hand quilted by*
*Rose Augenstein.*

# Series:
# TRAMP ART
# (1983-      )

The TRAMP ART series is based on my interpretation of my collection of Tramp Art which consists of small boxes, chests and frames made of scraps of wood cut into geometric shapes and glued together. Cigar boxes were often used for the wood as they were easy to carve with a knife and could be found in the trash.

Tramp Art was made in the late 1880's by tramps in exchange for room and board. This art is highly eccentric.

❖ *(Left) Studio wall with TRAMP ART II and parts of the PASSION Series under construction. 1983. Photograph by Nancy Crow.*

❖ *(Below) TRAMP ART II, ©Nancy Crow, 1983, (47½" x 26½"), hand quilted by Mrs. Levi Mast. Collection of Christina Bigler, Switzerland. Photograph by Nancy Crow.*

❖ *(Below)*
*PASSION II,*
*©Nancy Crow,*
*1984, (48" x 48"),*
*hand quilted by*
*Rose Augenstein.*

# Series: PASSION (1983-1985)

The PASSION Series consists of only five quilts all done as a memorial to my mother, Rachel Kensett Crow. In May of 1983 she entered the hospital to have knee-replacement surgery which was successful. However, two weeks later while undergoing physical therapy, she suffered a massive stroke that put her into a coma until November 1984, when she died. Those 18 months of sorrowing for her and watching her slowly die made me re-examine my motives about why I was making quilts. Life seemed so joyless, so harsh, so graphic, that my color usage dwindled down to black, white, red and blue predominantly. I was depressed. I could not bring myself to use color until PASSION V. PASSION V contains lots of colors, sparkling colors, because it came after Mother had died, and I began to feel again a sense of purpose and happiness. I "needed" to make a quilt that appeared joyful and hopeful.

The center of PASSION IV (as shown on the right in the photo below) was actually begun first before any of the other PASSION quilts, but I could not finish it until 1985 just before I made PASSION V.

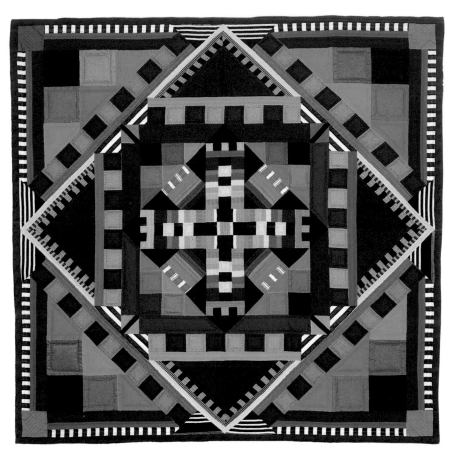

❖ *(Right) Blocks*
*for PASSION I*
*being developed*
*on wall of studio*
*(in front parlor of*
*the house) with the*
*center of PASSION*
*IV to the right.*
*1984. Photograph*
*by Nancy Crow.*

❖ *(Above)  PASSION I,*
*©Nancy Crow, 1984,*
*(70" x 70"), hand quilted*
*by Amish quilting bee,*
*Holmes County, Ohio.*
*Collection of Abbe Cheek,*
*Ohio.*

❖ *(Above)*
*PASSION III,*
*©Nancy Crow,*
*1985, (85" x 85"),*
*hand quilted by*
*Mrs. Jacob*
*Hershberger.*

PASSION III was the last quilt that I made in my studio in the house. After finishing it, I moved into my new studio that stands just outside my kitchen door.

Both PASSION III and PASSION IV incorporate motifs used in the TRAMP ART Series.

❖ *(Above)*
*PASSION IV,*
*©Nancy Crow,*
*1984-1985,*
*(84" x 84"),*
*hand quilted by*
*Rose Augenstein.*

❖ *(Right)*
*PASSION V in beginning stages of construction on the wall of my new studio, a renovated 130-year-old barn.*

❖ *(Below)*
*PASSION V in advanced stages of construction. I had to use a ladder because of the quilt's huge size. And I had to walk outside the studio and look in the front glass doors to get enough distance to make sure the composition was working. Although my new studio is 25 feet long, that is still not enough distance for something over 8 feet square in size.*

I spent nearly two weeks just strip-piecing combinations of fabrics that I then cut up again and resewed to make all the checkered areas. When sewing such a large quilt together, the growing weight of the fabrics causes a lot of strain and stress to the shoulders and across one's upper back. It's a killer!

❖ *(Above) PASSION V,
©Nancy Crow, 1985,
(102" x 102"), hand
quilted by Amish
quilting bee. Holmes
County, Ohio.*

# Series: YELLOW CROSSES (1985)

I was emotionally burnt-out when I started this series in 1985 and was not even sure I could go through another new struggle to make a quilt. Instinctively I felt I had to start over again and start out simply. I knew I had to work with crosses so I decided each quilt in the series would start with a simple structure of yellow crosses. I used as many yellow and gold fabrics as I had collected over the years, and cut out long narrow rectangles and pinned them up on the wall to form crosses. Just putting up these simple crosses to indicate the final size of each quilt was therapeutic. I let them stay there . . . solitary . . . for several days so I could react to their shapes against the white spaces of the wall behind. I remember thinking that the colors were so lush, so warm, but I wanted the crosses to symbolize the burdens that people must bare during their lifetimes. Burdens of sorrow, burdens of fear, burdens of guilt, burdens of all types. YELLOW CROSSES I and II represent burdens of sorrow for me, the burden of witnessing the agonizingly long and slow death of my mother. In the face of her impending death my quiltmaking seemed totally frivolous and

ridiculous. Too selfish. I had almost decided to quit making quilts before I started the YELLOW CROSSES Series.

In one way, the yellow crosses form the bars of a prison wall with all the rich variety of life repressed beneath. Not until I made YELLOW CROSSES IV was I able to bring that life from underneath up through the bars, blending it with the yellows and finally letting it transcend them.

In YELLOW CROSSES I and II, I used the simplest of templates. I began both of these quilts at the same time, side by side on the front studio wall. (Refer to photograph on next page showing the two quilts.) I decided ahead that YELLOW CROSSES I would be developed from pastel solids and prints while YELLOW CROSSES II would become a solid color study with only a small amount of strip-piecing in it. I did not want strip-piecing to absorb me.

In YELLOW CROSSES I, I wanted to mimic the fabrics my mother used in her house dresses that she wore everyday when I was a child. Those old-fashioned yellow and white kitchen checks, strange seersuckers and funny pastel plaids.

❖ *(Right)*
*My mother,*
*Rachel Crow*
*(age 50), 1949,*
*standing behind*
*my brother,*
*Andrew, and me.*

❖ (Above)
YELLOW CROSSES
I, ©Nancy Crow,
1985, (82" x 82"),
hand quilted by
two sisters, Sarah
Hershberger and
Mrs. John E. Mast.

❖ (Overleaf)
Interior of studio
showing YELLOW
CROSSES I and II
hanging side by
side. 1985.
Photograph by
Nancy Crow.

❖ *(Below) YELLOW
CROSSES II, detail.*

❖ *(Above) YELLOW CROSSES II, ©Nancy Crow, 1985, (78" x 78"), hand quilted by Rose Augenstein.*

When I began YELLOW CROSSES III, I used a much larger block that was 30" square. Again I cut out the crosses first and pinned them up on the wall (refer to photo below). I decided to explore even greater simplicity . . . just huge blocks of solid colors, mostly blues laid in under the yellows. I used black and white to create bold life around the outside edges. In hindsight I think this quilt truly shows how repressed I was feeling.

❖ (Above) YELLOW CROSSES III in progress, 1985. Photograph by Nancy Crow.

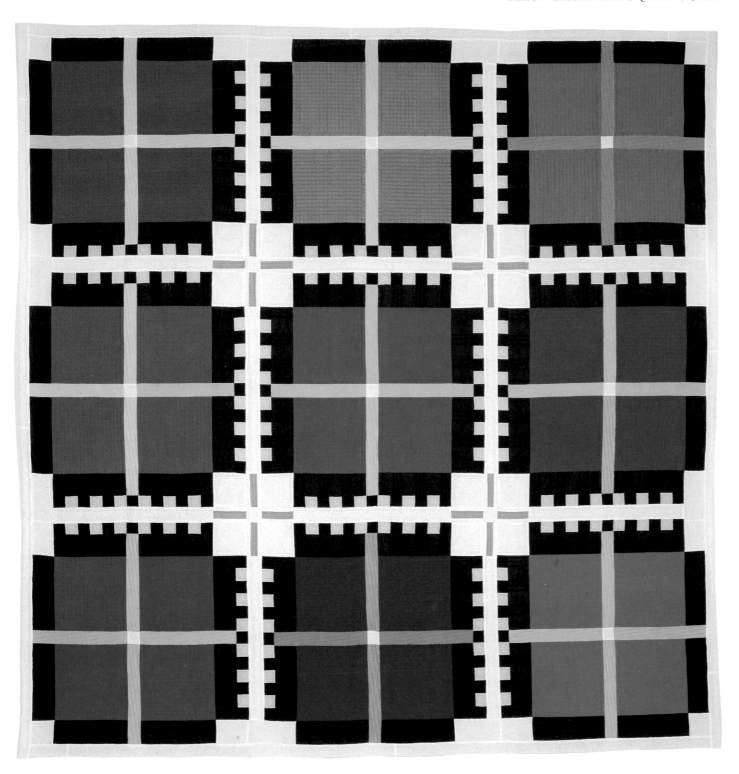

❖ *(Above)*
*YELLOW CROSSES*
*III, ©Nancy Crow,*
*1985, (96" x 96"),*
*hand quilted by*
*Rose Augenstein.*

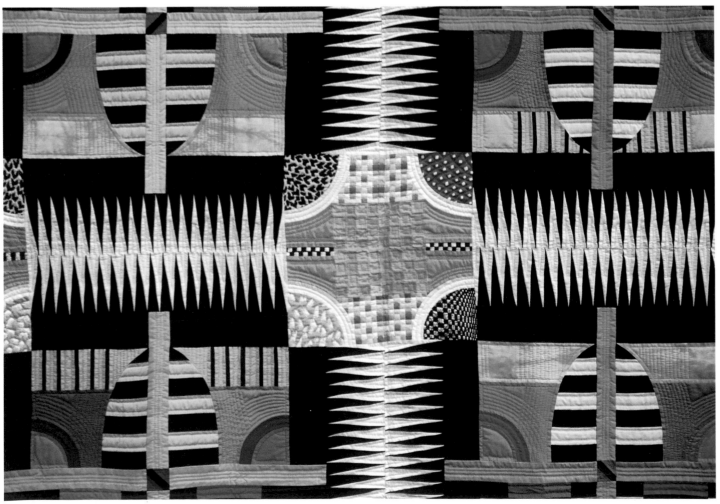

❖ *(Top on page 152) YELLOW CROSSES IV in progress. 1985. Photograph by Nancy Crow.*

❖ *(Bottom on page 152) YELLOW CROSSES IV in progress. 1985. Photograph by Nancy Crow.*

❖ *(Top on page 153) YELLOW CROSSES IV in progress. 1985. Photograph by Nancy Crow.*

❖ *(Bottom on page 153) YELLOW CROSSES IV in progress. 1985. Photograph by Nancy Crow.*

❖ *(Right) YELLOW CROSSES IV hanging in the exhibit, "Poetry Of The Physical," at the American Craft Museum, New York City. 1986.*

❖ *(Opposite page) YELLOW CROSSES IV, ©Nancy Crow, 1985, (82" x 82"), hand quilted by Mrs. Dan Raber. Collection of Elizabeth and Mark Levine. Photograph by Nancy Crow.*

With the start of YELLOW CROSSES IV, I needed to break loose. To shout with joy. "To let go of FEAR." To let what would happen, happen . . . and it did! It all came tumbling out! I made new templates to accommodate the strange shapes, and I experimented with color. I realize now that this quilt documents my coming to grips with the deep fear I always felt about bees. When I was very young our neighbor's backyard was filled with beehives, a no-man's land. Danger! I hated crossing over into their yard. The beehives were five across and seven deep down the whole slope of their backyard. During summertime, those bee's were thick everywhere. There was no

avoiding being stung over and over again. My brother, Andrew, unlike me and fearless, tried to knock the beehives over when he was six years old. At some point I overcame my fears and went through the barriers. YELLOW CROSSES IV is "the coming through," bees and all. Yes, I also have a sense of humor!

In 1986, Paul J. Smith, director of the American Craft Museum in New York City, chose YELLOW CROSSES IV to be included in the exhibition "Craft Today: Poetry Of The Physical." The exhibition commemorated the opening of the Museum's new building at 40 West 53rd Street, New York City, directly across the street from the Museum of Modern Art.

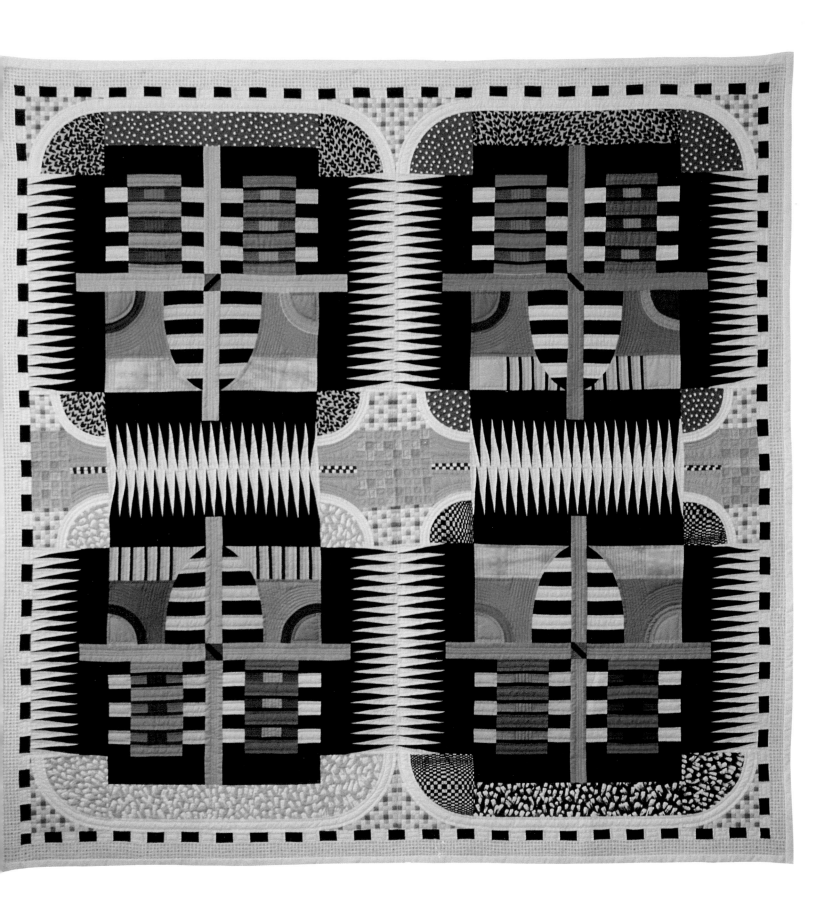

❖ *(Above) IN
HOMAGE,
©Nancy Crow,
1986, (85" x 85"),
hand quilted by
Rose Augenstein.*

For several years, I taught a class in quiltmaking to children ages 10-16, as part of the creative arts program in 4-H. My son, Matthew, who was part of this group, machine-pieced his first quilt at age 10. He has designed and machine-pieced six tops so far.

❖ *(Above) LEAVES, ©Matthew Crow Stitzlein, 1986, (92" x 92"), designed and machine pieced by Matthew Crow Stitzlein, age 14. Hand quilted by Peg Ries.*

# Series: LADY OF GUADALUPE

❖ *(Top left) PORTRAIT OF WOMAN WITH CARNATIONS, a painting by Vincent Van Gogh, 1887. Collection of The Louvre, Paris, France. This painting inspired the first LADY OF GUADALUPE. I saw log-cabin patterning in the skirt and a yellow halo in the background.*

❖ *(Top right) LADY OF GUADALUPE I in progress, 1985. Photograph by Nancy Crow.*

❖ *(Below) Studio interior showing LADY OF GUADALUPE I in progresss. Photograph by Nancy Crow.*

❖ *(Opposite page) LADY OF GUADALUPE I, © Nancy Crow, 1985, (57½" x 82"), hand quilted by Sarah Hershberger. This quilt is included in the book,* The Art Quilt, *by Penny McMorris and Michael Kile, and has traveled in an exhibit titled, "The Art Quilt," from 1986-1989, to various museums around the United States.*

I began the LADY OF GUADALUPE Series for several reasons. At age 19, I lived in Mexico City and studied art at Mexico City College. While there I became familiar with this Saint and her symbolism. I was fascinated by the idea of "goodness" radiating out from and around the form of OUR LADY. In 1985, I felt a real need to produce quilts that reflected a sense of "goodness." I have made five quilts in this series and plan many more.

❖ (Right) I began
LADY OF
GUADALUPE II by
first pinning up on
the front studio
wall the four
different blocks-to-
size that I planned
to use. I studied
those blocks
drawn on
tagboard until I
began to learn
visually the size of
each template.
Then I cut some of
the templates out
of printed fabrics
to try to get a sense
of how the quilt
might begin to
develop. I also
pinned up some
fabrics to the right
as inspiration,
only to discard
them about a
month later. I left
this framework up
for three months
before getting the
idea of making
textured-looking
strip-piecing in
gradations. It took
me two solid weeks
of sewing just to
make all the strip-
pieced fabrics.
Photograph  by
Nancy Crow.

❖ (Bottom right)
Some of the 20
odd new fabrics I
constructed for
LADY OF
GUADALUPE II.
I used many
different
gradations set
between "textured-
looking" prints.

❖ (Left) The structure of the quilt is slowly growing after the gradated strip-pieced fabrics have been "laid in." Those fabrics helped direct the development of the rest of the quilt. Photograph by Nancy Crow.

❖ (Below left) The black and white Merimekko fabrics pinned to the right on the wall were "one of those great finds." I cut out the floating feathers and sewed them together to form part of the halo for the LADY OF GUADALUPE II. The simple color structure pinned to the left is the beginning of the LADY OF GUADALUPE III. Photograph by Nancy Crow.

❖ (Page 162-163) Interior view of studio with the LADY OF GUADA-LUPE II under construction. Photograph by Nancy Crow.

❖ (Page 164) Detail of the LADY OF GUADALUPE II, ©Nancy Crow.

❖ (Page 165) LADY OF GUADALUPE II, ©Nancy Crow, 1986-87 (64" x 80"), hand quilted by Marla Hattabaugh.

❖ *(Right top) LADY OF GUADALUPE III in progress. 1987. Photograph by Nancy Crow.*

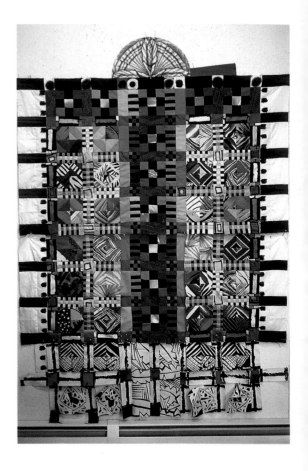

After using so many complicated blocks in making LADY OF GUADALUPE II, I felt I must simplify my templates. So I chose to use two differently sized squares and one rectangle. So all of LADY III was made using only three templates, with the exception of the semi-circles and radiating fan shapes at the top of the quilt. I used a multitude of printed fabrics for the dress. At the base of the dress, I cut up black and white prints and regrouped them, all the while thinking of them as a form of drawing, sketches at the base of her dress. In the radiating fan shapes at the top of the quilt, I used a 1950's cotton print that I found in a shop in Los Angeles, a shop that caters to the film industry and period costumes.

❖ *(Right) LADY OF GUADALUPE III in progress. 1987. Photograph by Nancy Crow.*

❖ *(Opposite page) LADY OF GUADALUPE III, ©Nancy Crow, 1987, (48" x 80"), hand quilted by Rose Augenstein. Photograph by Kevin Fitzsimons.*

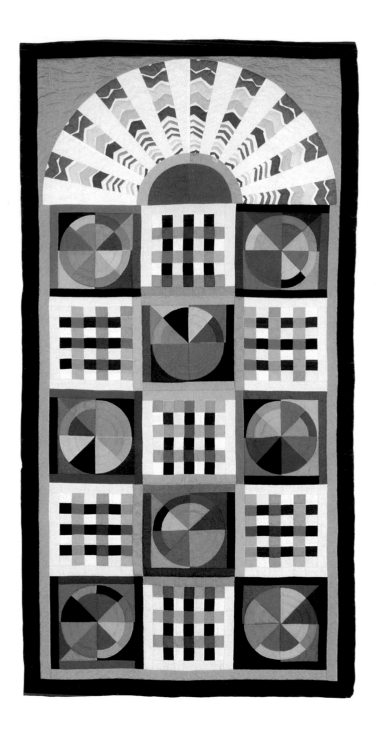

Both of these quilts were done as pure color studies with strip-piecing done only to make the grids.

❖ *(Right) LADY OF GUADALUPE IV, ©Nancy Crow, 1988, (34" x 64"), hand quilted by Marla Hattabaugh.*

❖ *(Left) LADY OF GUADALUPE V, ©Nancy Crow, 1988, (34" x 64"), hand quilted by Mrs. Levi Mast.*

# Series:
# JACOB'S LADDER
# (1986–    )

All the quilts in this series are essentially solid color studies using the old traditional block, Jacob's Ladder, as the basis. All three quilts are rectangles.

❖ *(Above) JACOB'S LADDER I in-progress. 1986. Photograph by Tom Holmes.*

❖ *(Above)*
*JACOB'S LADDER*
*I, ©Nancy Crow,*
*1986, (58" x 70"),*
*hand quilted by*
*Rose Augenstein.*
*Photograph by*
*Nancy Crow.*

171

❖ *(Above)*
*JACOB'S*
*LADDER II,*
*©Nancy Crow,*
*1986, (60" x 48"),*
*hand quilted by*
*Rose Augenstein.*
*Photograph by*
*Nancy Crow.*

❖ *(Above)*
*JACOB'S*
*LADDER III,*
*©Nancy Crow,*
*1987, (74" x 100"),*
*hand quilted by*
*Rose Augenstein.*

# Series:
# AMISH PAISLEY
# (1987-      )

❖ *(Right) Four different 10" blocks drawn out on tagboard to size, and joined together to form a 20" block which is the basis for this quilt, AMISH PAISLEY, in-progress. 1987.*

❖ *(Below) The same quilt and block as above, but seen from a distance. This quilt is being developed on my front studio wall which is the largest of my five working walls. It is 15' wide and 10' high and is covered in white celotex boards.*

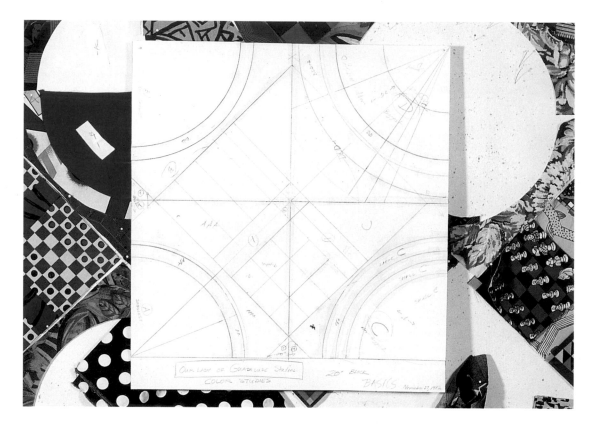

I began this quilt in 1987 as a form of protest against fabrics then available that used miniature copies of some of the wonderful old Amish quilts as motifs. I have a dear long-time Amish friend who has told me repeatedly how tired the Amish get of the "English" or non-Amish exploiting anything Amish to make money. As she has so often pointed out, there is no such thing as Amish cheese because the Amish do not make cheese.

In some ways, I felt these fabrics were a desecration of the historical Amish quilts. A few of the color-ways were even foreign to the colors the Amish used in their old quilts. In fact these color-ways were so ugly that I could not bring myself to use them. None of the imitation Amish fabrics that I bought were on the straight grain of the fabric, so the actual blocks that I cut out to use are quite crooked, and that is how they will stay in my own quilt.

Although I have not yet finished this quilt, I plan to break down the shapes even further, making it very, very complex. I will probably even elaborate on the title and call it AMISH PAISLEY WITH A MEXICAN TWIST! It is based on the same 10" block that I used in MEXICAN WHEELS I (page 183).

❖ *(Below)*
*AMISH PAISLEY*
*in-progress,*
*©Nancy Crow,*
*1987-.*

# Series:
# COLOR BLOCKS
# 1988-

The COLOR BLOCKS series was begun because of my need "to go back to just a few shapes and keep simple." I wanted to work with only a few templates, two differently sized squares and one small rectangle. I wanted those three templates to be set so that my variables could explore color and my new selection of wildly printed cottons.

In each quilt, I decided I would explore one color in depth so that it would predominate when viewed. So in COLOR BLOCKS I it is blue that predominates, while in COLOR BLOCKS II it is a combination of gray and blue. In COLOR BLOCKS III, which is currently under construction, I am exploring the widest range of yellows, yellow-greens, oranges and olive-greens that I have in my "fabric vocabulary."

I found a Merimekko fabric in New York City that I bought in four different color-ways and I am using it in the small rectangles as a given in each quilt. The design on the fabric gives a sense of iridescence from a distance, and I like that. At this point in my quilt making, I only want to use cottons and some blends. I am not interested in velvets, satins, nor lamé, but only the cottons, whether in wonderful solid colors or in smashing prints. I want the simplest of means to achieve the most glorious results. This is my dream.

❖ *(Opposite page) COLOR BLOCKS I, ©Nancy Crow, 1988, (62" x 62"), hand quilted by Elizabeth Miller. Collection of the artist.*

❖ *(Right) COLOR BLOCKS I under construction in the west 9' x 9' alcove of my studio. The center cross is made up of very small squares put together in nine patch formation. The fabrics are all cottons. Between the nine patches are rectangles of a Merimekko print. Photograph by Nancy Crow, 1988.*

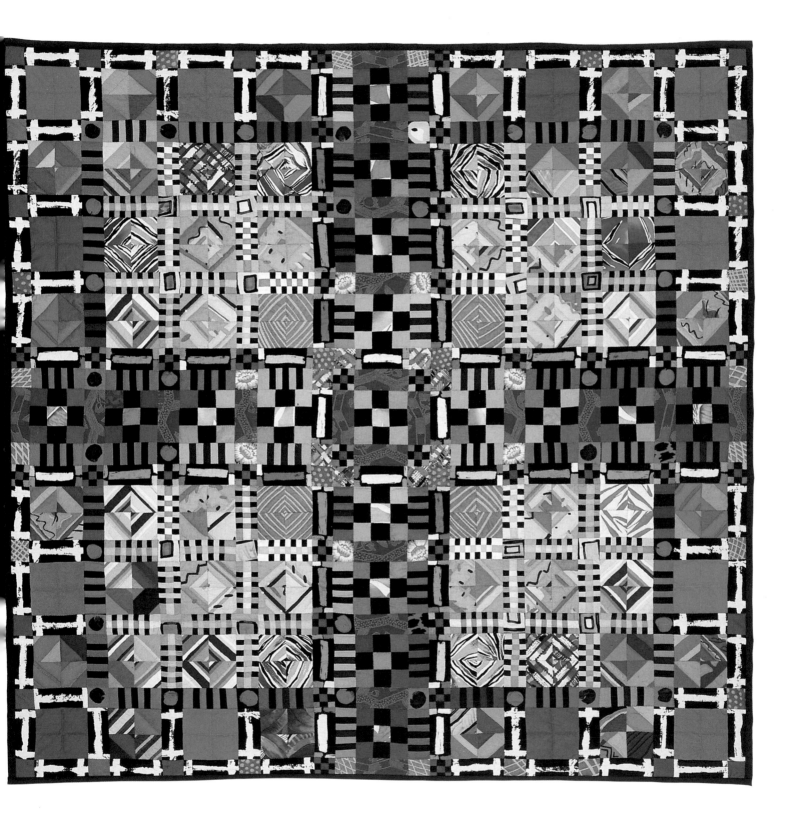

❖ *(Above)*
*COLOR BLOCKS II,*
*©Nancy Crow,*
*1988, (44" x 44"),*
*hand quilted by*
*Elizabeth Miller.*
*Collection of the*
*artist.*

❖ (Above) Many different shades of yellows and tans were stripped together with black to form a new fabric that was then cut, resewn, and cut again to fit the rectangular template. Also the rectangle was used with prints.

❖ (Left) Here I am using the smaller square templates to cut squares of fabric on the diagonal print, so that when they are sewn together, they form diamond shapes. Some of them turned out vague while others turned out strong.

❖ *COLOR BLOCKS III, ©Nancy Crow, under construction in the west 9' x 9' alcove. 1988-1989. This quilt is being developed intuitively. I have no working drawing of any sort. All of my quilts after 1978 have been made in this way, "intuitively", "to size," on the wall with much fabric wasted in the process. I must work this way making visual judgements as I move along. I hate working from a drawing. It is too constricting.*

# Series:
# MEXICAN WHEELS
# (1987–    )

❖ *(Right) A row of strip-pieced rectangles ready to be cut apart and used in MEXICAN WHEELS I. Top photographs by Nancy Crow.*

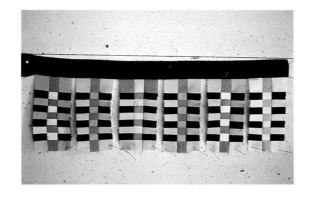

❖ *(Far right) The construction of the center of one of the quad-rants in MEXICAN WHEELS I.*

❖ *(Above) Nancy Crow working in her studio. Photograph by Kevin Fitzsimons. 1988.*

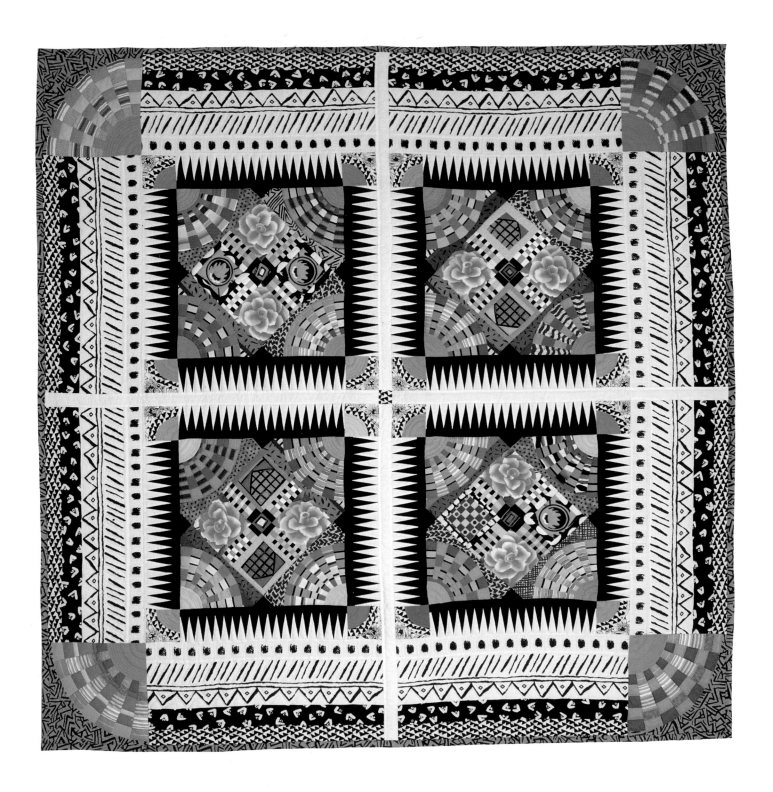

❖ *(Above)*
*MEXICAN*
*WHEELS I,*
*©Nancy Crow,*
*1987-88,*
*(82" x 82"), hand*
*quilted by Rose*
*Augenstein.*
*Chosen for Quilt*
*National '89.*

❖ *(Below &
opposite page)
Steps 1, 2, 3 and 4
in making
"points" quickly
and easily. I used
this method in
YELLOW CROSSES
IV, LADY OF
GUADALUPE II
and in MEXICAN
WHEELS I.*

I started the MEXICAN WHEELS series during the summer of 1987 and plan to continue with it. It is based on two things I love very much: Mexican culture and arts and the old quilt pattern called "New York Beauty." (Refer to pages 46-47).

In this series, part of my intention is to portray a sense of gaiety, a love of life and a sense of humor. Some of the iconography in Mexican life that has influenced me are the brightly painted spokes of oxen carts, the huge brilliant embroidered flowers on the Tehuana costumes from Oaxaca, and the crocheted lace that edges the necklines and cap sleeves of most peasant blouses. Even the basic structure of a blouse made up of squares and rectangles fascinates me. The engineering often creates wonderful patterns in the seam lines alone.

The border of MEXICAN WHEELS I and the cross in the center of MEXICAN WHEELS II are meant to be reminiscent of the crocheted lace, and that is why they are done in black and white. I have been collecting black and white fabrics for several years and keep them stacked on their own special shelves in my studio. I used five different black and white printed fabrics in the border of MEXICAN WHEELS I. By cutting them up and sewing them together, I tried to create the sense of airiness one might see in lace.

Technically the break-up of individual templates into smaller pieces either by piecing or strip-piecing took long hours. I worked on MEXICAN WHEELS I for six months. I was concerned with establishing the right scale in the strip-piecing to fit the size of the templates in the 10" block. When I switched to a 20" block for MEXICAN WHEELS II, I had to make much larger strip-piecing that was appropriate in size.

I could not have made either of these quilts in 1986 or earlier, as I simply did not have the fabrics. They were not available. But with the advent of "Jams!" Wow! Wonderful fabrics simply gushed forth nearly as fast as teenagers change their minds. I think that "Jams" caused a revolution in fabric designs and color combinations. This revolution caused me to "unload" an estimated $5,000.00 in order to buy this new "fabric vocabulary." The fabrics I bought were visually freeing to me. It was like being let out of prison.

I became overwhelmed by all the choices. It is so exciting to start new quilts knowing I have the raw materials to work with. Plus I own a huge selection of solids that I have been collecting since 1977. And the poor remaining calicoes? They languish on the shelf looking so forlorn. But they were the lucky ones as all the rest got cut into strips and were woven into rag rugs.

I must make clear that I would never have had such an incredible fabric selection if I did not travel and teach all over the United States and sometimes abroad. I try to go shopping for fabrics wherever I teach. I am sure I am remembered well by various hostesses since I am so single-minded! My energy levels reach new heights when there is the possibility of fabric shopping!

Today there are a number of companies producing fabrics of high quality not only in the gray goods, but in the printing, the designs and color combinations. These fabrics feel wonderful to touch. They stir up emotions. They inspire. And quiltmakers should be using this quality in their work. Extraordinary fabrics at reasonable prices are being produced by John Kaldor, Alexander Henry, Thompson of California, Hoffman, Midori, Merry Mary, Tandler Textiles, Gutcheon and Hamil Textiles. I also buy many unusual prints put out by Marcus Bros. and Liberty prints when I can get them on sale. I found one print I loved for $60.00 per yard. Too rich for my pocketbook, alas! The average price I have paid for these better fabrics is from $5.00 to $24.00 per yard and I look for sales whenever I can.

I have always made it a practice to wash any new purchased fabrics in the hottest of water with Tide detergent. The detergent will be sure to "move the dyes" if they are not fast. Over the years, I have learned which companies produce poorly dyed fabrics whose dyes often run. Sometimes the water will turn as dark as the dyed fabric itself. And it will take up to six to eight washings to get all the

excess dye out. At times, the dye simply will not stop running. Those fabrics will never be used in my quilts and represent wasted money. Money I threw away. And it makes me angry! I keep asking myself why should companies producing fabrics specifically for the quilt making market be so careless about quality control?

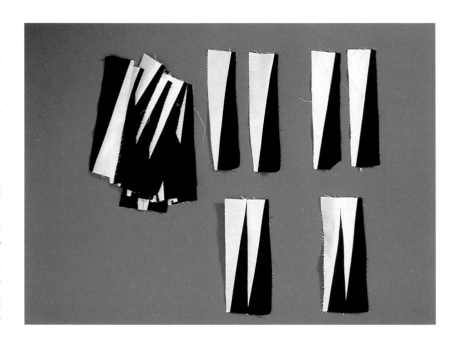

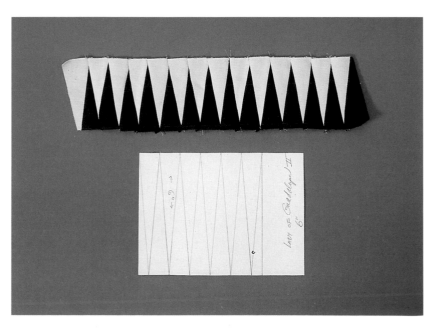

❖ *(Right)*
*MEXICAN TIGRE*
*MASKS. Collection*
*of Nancy Crow.*
*Photograph by*
*Nancy Crow,*
*1988.*

❖ *(Above)*
*MEXICAN*
*WHEELS II,*
*©Nancy Crow,*
*1988, (90" x 90"),*
*hand quilted by*
*Marie Moore.*
*Photograph by*
*Kevin Fitzsimons.*

# Series: DOUBLE MEXICAN WEDDING RINGS (1988–    )

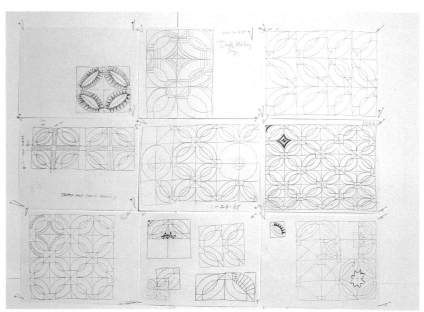

❖ *(Top right) Working out ideas with pencil sketches. 1988.*

❖ *(Center right) Using the new QUICKLINE II to draw the arcs for the 18" block used in DOUBLE WEDDING RINGS I. (The new QUICKLINE II has multiple holes for drawing any size arc and comes in three sizes: 12", 18", 24". Ordering information is at the back of book.)*

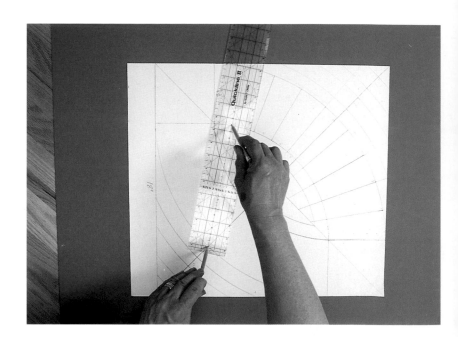

❖ *(Bottom right) Sewing the first strips together to form the new fabrics that will be used in this quilt. Photograph by Nancy Crow.*

❖ (Top left) The basic structure of DOUBLE MEXICAN WEDDING RINGS I has been established by laying in the positive/negative configuration "to-size." This is absolutely essential for me so that I can begin to visually orient myself to the graphic impact the quilt will have. I also need to make sure that the fundamental spatial relationships are dynamic before I begin. Photograph by Nancy Crow.

❖ (Bottom left) Leaving the black shapes and the gray shapes alone, I first developed the solid color areas that join the arcs together. Photograph by Nancy Crow.

❖ *(Top right) I have laid out all the templates I have made for the main arc to see how I can break this arc down into smaller components. I am very interested in using wedges. I eventually developed two different types of strip-piecing for these wedge templates as detailed in the photographs below. Photograph by Nancy Crow.*

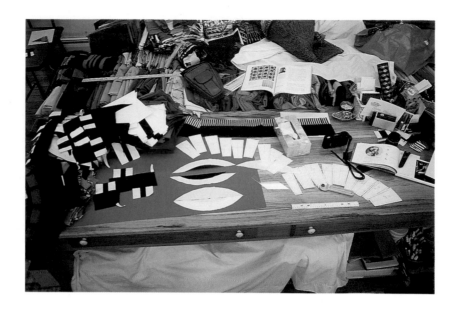

❖ *(Center right) The first type of strip-piecing has been made, and I am cutting off 2½" sections (using QUICKLINE II) that I will sew onto the black strip as shown to the left of my hand. After I have sewn these sections onto the black fabric strip, I lay on the wedge template, trace around it, and cut out the shapes. I then sew all the wedges together to form the main arc shape as shown at top in this picture.*

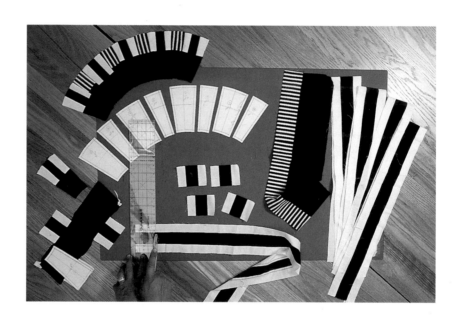

❖ *(Bottom right) The second type of finished strip-piecing lays to the right and at the bottom, the wedge template has been positioned on one piece of the new strip-piecing. A sewn arc is in the upper left.*

190

❖ *(Left) I have begun replacing solid black arcs with strip-pieced arcs and I am beginning to get a sense of the energy I hope this quilt will generate. Photograph by Nancy Crow.*

❖ *(Below) Now, I am working on the solid gray arcs too. But I have not sewn any of the blocks together yet as I want to try the blocks in other configurations first. Photograph by Nancy Crow.*

❖ *(Above and Right) Turning of the blocks of DOUBLE MEXICAN WEDDING RINGS I into other formations just to see what might result.*
*Photographs by Nancy Crow.*

❖ *(Left) Turning of the blocks of DOUBLE MEXICAN WEDDING RINGS I into one last formation before deciding to put them back into the traditional formation of the old Double Wedding Rings. 1988. Photograph by Nancy Crow.*

❖ *(Below) The final sewing together of the blocks into DOUBLE MEXICAN WEDDING RINGS I. ©Nancy Crow, 1988. Photograph by Nancy Crow.*

❖ *(Right)*
*DOUBLE MEXICAN*
*WEDDING RINGS I,*
*detail.*

❖ *(Below)*
*The back of*
*DOUBLE MEXICAN*
*WEDDING RINGS I,*
*(72" x 72"),*
*showing the*
*quilting pattern.*
*Hand quilted by*
*Marie Moore. 1988.*

❖ *(Above)*
*DOUBLE MEXICAN*
*WEDDING RINGS I,*
*©Nancy Crow, 1988,*
*(72" x 72"), hand quilted*
*by Marie Moore.*

# SADIE CHESROWN (1898-1986)

❖ *(Top right) Sadie Chesrown standing in front of her house.*

❖ *(Below) Sadie's house. Sadie and my mother, Rachel Crow, standing together.*

❖ *(Opposite top) The living room of Sadie's house showing red glow from wallpaper.*

❖ *(Opposite middle) The nude drawings that cover the walls of the upstairs bathroom.*

❖ *(Opposite bottom) Sadie's kitchen sink with collage of President Reagan over it.*

*All photographs were taken by Nancy Crow.*

Sadie Chesrown, a widow, lived on a farm northeast of Loudonville. She and her husband, Todd, and their six children had been long-time friends with our family. Sadie's children grew up with my

older sisters and brothers and Sadie was close to my mother in age.

I loved to go to Sadie's. Her house was full of art: Art on the walls and in the making, watercolors underway on the easel, a dress cut out ready to be sewn, crocheting laying on the couch, a rug loom taking up a huge section of the kitchen and later part of her bedroom.

Her floors were covered with wall-to-wall rag rugs that she had woven out of strips from worn clothing. "She was the mistress of 'make-do'," says one of her daughters, BeBee Curry. "As a child, I always knew there was nothing she couldn't do."

She and Todd took four to five years to cover their frame house with bricks, brick by brick by themselves. She was tiny, only about five feet tall, and rail thin, but she was willing to tackle any job and did what had to be done. They tore out the original doors leading from one room to another, widened the doorways and encased and supported the floors above with massive solid cherry beams that had been cut out of their own woods.

When she was in her 50's she tore down the walls of her old kitchen and rebuilt the new one by herself, with the shape and design that she wanted. When I asked her how she knew how to renovate and build a new kitchen, she replied, "You just do it!" She kept her old wood-burning stove because she preferred to cook on it.

She attended the Cleveland School of Art (now the Cleveland Art Institute) from 1918-1922, where she studied painting. After her marriage and move to the farm, she painted watercolors of the life around her. From her days in art school she brought with her a stack of nude drawings of both men and women. Since she did not believe in wasting anything and with her incredible sense of humor, she papered the wall of her upstairs bathroom with the nudes, and with what was left over, papered one wall of her sitting room downstairs. She had many a good laugh over that decision!

When she was in her late 70's or early 80's she decided to paper her walls and ceiling with a red print wallpaper. The effect of the red made the whole house glow. (As you can see in the accompanying photograph). She wanted none of that "old ladies" type of decorating!

One day when I visited her, I found a new collage mounted just over the sink in her kitchen. It showed the head and shoulders of President Reagan, several huge birds, flowers and a mix of insects flying around. She laughed and told me it was her way of showing that "he had butterflies in the brain!" She was 83.

She was eccentric. She was original. She was adamant about nature. Loved nature. "Always believed that nature held the only truth," states BeBee. She protected

her farm and chased away hunters with a shotgun saying, "I'm not afraid of them."

For a companion after she was widowed, she dressed a mannequin with one of her own dresses and one of her scarves tied around its hair, and put the mannequin in a rocking chair near the window. She named her "Sally DoLittle!" Sally's job was to make it look like someone was in the house in case anyone peeked through

the window. Sadie sometimes placed yarn and needles in her hands so it would look like she was knitting. Or she would have her reading the newspaper. I even saw her holding the rolls of wallpaper when Sadie had her house wallpapered.

Sally DoLittle now occupies a space in my upstairs office. When I first got her, I forgot she was sitting in a chair and when I would run upstairs to answer the phone in my office, I would nearly drop dead from fright. It was totally unnerving to have a life-size figure sitting up there. Now Sally is a comfort.

BeBee says that, "Sadie always emphasized being an individual and would admonish her children by saying, 'Be yourself! Don't be afraid to be different!'"

Since she never learned to drive a car and since the garage just stood there unused, she decided to paint a scene on the doors. (Accompanying photograph.)

And when she felt too tired to make a vegetable garden far from the house, she simply moved it up to the flower beds by the front steps. There by her front door she grew sweet corn, tomatoes and squash. She baked her own bread up to the last for she always said her favorite food was a slice of good bread.

I will never forget her image, her strong personality . . . standing there with silver bangles on her wrist, her turban in place, her long skirt to mid-calf, holding one of her happy, interesting conversations.

❖ *(Left) Sadie Chesrown enjoying a quiet moment. Photo courtesy of Chic Knight, Ashland Times-Gazette, 1979, Ashland, Ohio.*

❖ *(Below) Scene painted by Sadie Chesrown on her garage door. Photograph by Nancy Crow.*

# INFLUENCES:

❖ *(Above) A set of ten graduated split white oak market baskets made by Gertie Youngblood. Collection of Nancy Crow.*

# THINGS-IN-A-ROW

❖ *(Below) Two sets of graduated grain measuring baskets, one set is old and the other new, from Upper Volta. Collection of Nancy Crow.*

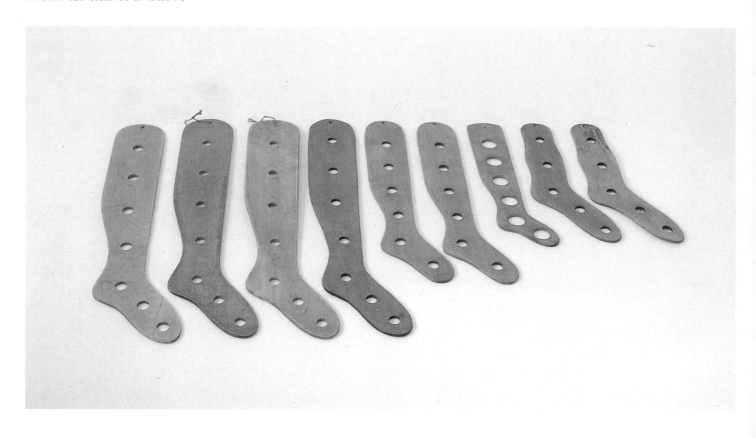

❖ *(Top on both pages)*
*Wooden stocking stretchers*
*used to shape knitted stockings.*
*Collection of Nancy Crow.*

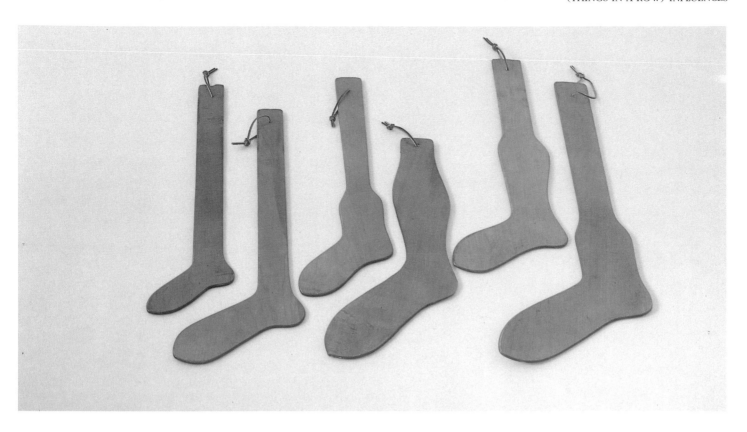

❖ *(Below on both pages)*
*An iron and wooden fence.*
*Photograph by Nancy Crow.*

❖ *(Overleaf) Things-In-A-Row,*
*four different photographs*
*by Nancy Crow.*

# THINGS-IN-A-ROW

# DOORS

All of the photographs of doors were taken in 1987 in Austria and West Germany except for the last photograph. I saw that door in Amsterdam in 1979.

Doors represent "taking risks." If one does not open the door, one can never go through and find out what is there; what could be; what might have happened. They are also mysterious to me, especially the ones shown here.

# DOORS

# DOORS

# COLOR

All photographs in the Color chapter were taken by Nancy Crow.

❖ (Left) Trellis in West Germany, 1987.

# COLOR

❖ *(Above) Amish buggies. Holmes County, Ohio. 1982.*

❖ (Above)
Floating Pansy.
1978.

# COLOR

❖ *(Above) Scene in Nova Scotia fishing village. 1985.*

❖ *(Above) Window in Austria. 1987.*

# COLOR

❖ *(Above) An Oriental Poppy, or Papaver in my front yard. 1988.*

❖ *(Above) Gold*
*Daylily. 1985.*

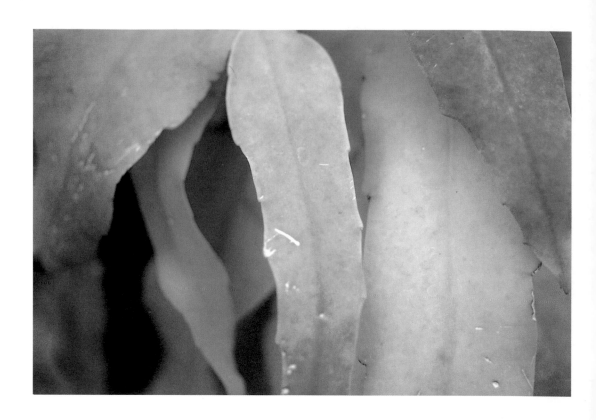

❖ *All photographs on pages 218 and 219 were taken by Nancy Crow during the time period of 1982-1988.*

# COLOR

❖ *(This page) All photographs were taken by Nancy Crow during the time period of 1979-1988.*

# COLOR

❖ *(This page)*
*All photographs*
*were taken by*
*Nancy Crow*
*during the time*
*period of*
*1979-1984.*

# TRAMP ART

❖ *(Below) Tramp Art table made from dynamite boxes from Atlas Powder Co. 34 wide, 33" high, 10½" deep.*

❖ *(Opposite right) Tramp Art chest of drawers. 33" high, 13½" wide, 8½" deep.*

❖ *(Opposite at top) Detail of inset on side of chest. Made of cigar boxes.*

All of the Tramp Art on this page and the next three are in the collection of Nancy Crow. Dates range from the late 1800's to 1943.

# TRAMP ART

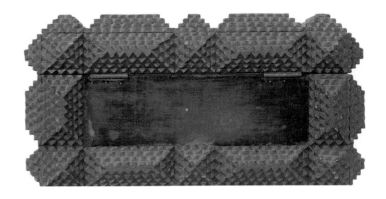

❖ *(Above)*
*Tramp Art box.*
*12" wide, 9" high*
*and 7" deep.*
*Says "MOTHER"*
*on handle.*

❖ *(Far Right)*
*Tramp Art box.*
*11½" wide,*
*6" tall and*
*8½" deep.*

❖ *(Right)*
*Tramp Art sewing*
*box dated 1943.*
*17" wide, 17" high*
*and 6" deep.*

❖ *(Left)*
*Tramp Art frame.*
*17" high,*
*11" wide.*

❖ *(Below)*
*Tramp Art chest*
*of drawers. 29"*
*high, 15½" wide*
*and 9½" deep.*

# WHIRLIGIGS

❖ *(Above) Wood and metal Whirligig with ferris wheel, a jogger, two men on a seesaw and one man riding a horse. 1982. 5 ft. long. Made by Norville Ault. Collection of Nancy Crow.*

❖ *(Right) Whirligig constructed of painted wood (cypress) blades. 1985. Made by John Adkins of Ullin, Illinois. Collection of Nancy Crow. Photograph by Nancy Crow.*

❖ *(Left) Whirligigs on the farm of John Adkins, Ullin, Illinois. They are made of bicycle wheels, painted chlorox bottles, plastic pop bottles, and anti-freeze containers, all cut off and screwed onto the metal rims. When I visited John Adkins' farm in December 1984, he had placed his whirligigs in every part of his yard and all around the house. They could be seen from a distance when driving up his lane. Photograph by Nancy Crow.*

❖ *(Bottom left) John Adkins, the folk artist, standing beside one of his whirligigs. He was 80 years old when this photograph was taken in 1985, in Ullin, Illinois. Mr. Adkins impressed me as.a man who loved making these whirligigs "out of throw-aways," and who had no idea how incredibly "inventive" he really was. He struck me as being very kind, and very gentle with a sense of humor. He was still farming in 1985 and making the whirligigs during the winter months. Photograph by Nancy Crow.*

# WHIRLIGIGS

❖ (Above) House
surrounded by
whirligigs with
some on the roof!
State of
Washington.
Photograph by
Nancy Crow.

❖ *(Left) Whirligigs fill the backyard. Painted tubs out of discarded washing machines are planted with petunias and make a line along the fence. State of Washington. Photograph by Nancy Crow.*

# WHIRLIGIGS

All the whirligigs on these facing pages were photographed in 1978 in the State of Washington, around the same house as seen in the preceding two pages. Among all the moving whirligigs, I saw an elderly couple patiently painting one of the whirligigs. I could not get their attention, so I do not know whose home this is or who made all of these colorful whirligigs.

My fondest wish is to someday have my own home and farm surrounded by whirligigs!

# ARTIFACTS

❖ *(Right) Head made of painted gourds. 1977. Pueblo Indians, Arizona. Collection of Nancy Crow. Photograph by Nancy Crow.*

❖ *(Opposite page) Jivaro Indian costume from Ecuador. Painted cloth made from bark with parts of Toucans sewn on. Decorated front and back. Collection of Nancy Crow.*

❖ (Top right)
Carved wooden
baby carrier from
Indonesia.
Collection of
Nancy Crow.

❖ (Below right)
Dowry box from
Indonesia made of
bamboo and
leaves. Earth
colored dyes and
sliced cowry shells
used for
decoration.
Collection of
Nancy Crow.

❖ (Opposite page)
Carved gourds
from Columbia and
Ecuador, South
America. Collection
of Nancy Crow.

# ARTIFACTS

# BASKETS

❖ *(Above)*
*CHITIMACHA*
*basket made by*
*Ada Thomas, a*
*Chitimacha*
*Indian from*
*Louisiana. Made*
*of finely prepared*
*strips of swamp-*
*cane dyed with*
*vegetable dyes.*
*Doubleweave.*
*1981.*

❖ *(Right)*
*Collection of*
*HOOPA (HUPA)*
*twined baskets.*
*Circa late 1880's,*
*California. These*
*are Lower*
*Klamath River*
*style with the*
*designs showing*
*only on the*
*outside. The*
*baskets are known*
*as "cap-hats."*

❖ (Above)
One of the
"masterpiece"
quality baskets
made by Mildred
Youngblood.
Considered one of
our finest native
basketmakers,
Mildred was able
to split white oak
to extremely fine
splints of only
quarter inch
width. 1981.
Woodbury,
Tennessee.

# BASKETS

All four baskets on these two pages are from China, Ning Po, Che-Kiang. They are doubleweave, made of plaited bamboo with carved bamboo handles on the lower two baskets. The basket in the upper right corner on the opposite page has been painted with so much red and black lacquer, that it is difficult to see the plaiting. Circa late 1890"s to early 1900's. Collection of Nancy Crow.

❖ (Right) Old bamboo grain storage basket from the Philippines. Collection of Nancy Crow.

240

❖ *(Left)*
*Lidded basket from China, Ning-Po, Che-Kiang. It is made of bamboo using techniques of plaiting and wickerwork. Collection of Nancy Crow.*

❖ *(Below)*
*The same basket as above but showing interior designs. Notice the inside of the lid is doubleweave and that the bamboo strips are not nearly so fine as those worked on the outside of the lid.*

# BASKETS

❖ *(Above)*
*Bottom of*
*Chinese basket*
*showing intricate*
*weave of bamboo*
*wicker over red*
*silk cloth. This is*
*the bottom of the*
*lidded basket on*
*preceding page.*

❖ *(Right) Spokes of*
*wood. Photograph*
*by Nancy Crow.*

❖ *(Below)*
*Part of my basket*
*collection after*
*being hosed off*
*and left to dry on*
*the grass.*
*Photograph by*
*Nancy Crow.*
*1988.*

# THAT TREE

THAT TREE is a wild cherry tree, perhaps 50 years old, that stands in the fence row between our farm and our neighbor's. It is majestic, uncomplaining, always there, a true beacon of friendship. It has sustained me over and over again through periods of sadness and loneliness. I have come to rely on it. I can see it from my kitchen windows. But only two weeks ago just after I took the large photo on the facing page, three men from the telephone company came and "hacked" off the ends of all the branches on the left side of the tree because they were "touching" their telephone pole . . . that ugly pole! All in the name of progress? Or efficiency? Now the "stubs" can no longer sway in the wind.

# THAT TREE

# OTHER TREES

❖ *All photographs in this book by Nancy Crow were taken over a 23 year period using a Nikon FM body with 55mm Micro-Nikkor lenses (both 3.5 and 2.8), with Koda-chrome ASA 64 film or ASA 25 film.*

I woke up Sunday morning November 13, 1988, and saw this view out of my window. It was 7:00 a.m.

I thought about when I was a child and stared out my upstairs bedroom window at the branches of the huge Norway maple growing in our backyard. I loved that tree. Every night I traced different patterns on the sky with those black branches. That tree was one of my first teachers.

And here 30 years later, outside my bedroom window are the branches of a young tree just starting to grow and change and form patterns with the sky. And I will grow and change too.

*Photograph by Nancy Crow.*

# Acknowledgments

I have been very fortunate in having the support and love of a very hard-working and understanding husband, John Stitzlein. He has been assisted many times by our two teenage sons, Nathaniel John Stitzlein and Matthew Crow Stitzlein. All three have helped with completing my studio, with packing quilts off to exhibitions, with cutting sticks for hanging quilts, with washing, ironing and folding fabrics and with marking quilt tops. I have truly been thankful for their sense of humor and their faith in me.

I also want to express my gratitude to all of my seven sisters and brothers spread out over the United States. All are very creative people who have been an inspiration to me.

I an indebted to The Ohio Quilt Research Group for having done much of the footwork in finding many of the fine old quilts of Ashland County that I have included in my book. On the day Jean and Carol photographed these quilts we were assisted by Ann and Noel Shaffer, Norma and Robert Snyder, Janice Kick, Bessie Hoyer, Thelma Portz, Elnora Snyder, Mozelle Fulmer, Marianne Winters, Celia Paullin and Peggy Young, all of Loudonville, Ohio. The photography took place in the Cleo Redd Fisher Museum, Loudonville. The Museum is a fascinating place to visit with treasures that include folk art, period rooms, period clothing, coverlets, quilts, dolls, button collections and antique furnishings.

Teachers have been very important in my life and I want to acknowledge the following: Marjorie Robinson, my high school English teacher who never expected less than the best; Mrs. Clifford Leach who taught creative writing; Harriet Beem, Loudonville's librarian when I was in high school. I worked under her and learned about "quality;" Edgar Littlefield, Professor, who told me I was talented enough to major in ceramics my junior year at Ohio State, and from whom I learned alot about being disciplined and especially about "respecting one's materials"; Professor Eugene Friley for guiding me through my M.F.A. program in ceramics, allowing me alot of freedom and for believing in me! Professor Paul Bogatay for giving my work such tough critiques in graduate school that I learned how to critique my own work and expect only the best from myself; Mary Ruth Pappenthien, my textiles professor, who posed some of the most intelligent, difficult and abstract design problems that one came to realize that one must work from one's own experience and that "there are no formulas in art." I salute her for projecting so much "passion" for textiles through words, poetry, actions and body movements . . . I was fascinated by her. I credit James Baughman in textiles when I was an undergraduate for letting me know "it was all right to applique and embroider" . . . they too can be art. And last I give my affection to Professor Margaret Fetzer in ceramics, for her honesty, wit, immense wealth of information, for listening to us all, for caring about us and helping us whenever . . . especially with technical problems.

I want to thank the following for encouraging my career: Danny Butts, Director of The Mansfield Art Center, Ohio; Jon Wahling, Head of Textiles at the Columbus, Ohio Cultural Arts Center; Wayne Lawson, Director, and The Ohio Arts Council for all the grants; JoAnn and Hal Stevens, Directors and The Ohio Designer Craftsmen for their dedication in promoting textiles and other arts in Ohio and nationwide; Governor and Dagmar Celeste for their wonderful support of the arts in Ohio and especially quilts; Robert Bishop, Director, of the Museum of American Folk Art, New York City; and finally to Paul J. Smith, Director Emeritus, and the American Craft Museum, New York City, for their strong support of contemporary quiltmaking.

I have been fortunate in having long-time friends who love quiltmaking as fiercely as I do: Michael James, Esther Parkhurst, Sister Linda Fowler, Janet Page-Kessler, Virginia Randles, Francoise Barnes, Mary Jo Dalrymple, Pauline Burbidge, Terrie Mangat, David Walker, Jan Myers, Donna Stader, Catherine Anthony, Libby Lehman, and Mary Caldwell.

Last, thank you to all the women who have handquilted my tops over the past thirteen years, especially, Velma Brill of Cambridge, Ohio, Rose Augenstein of Florida, and Mrs. Levi Mast, Pennsylvania. These three women have handquilted the bulk of my quilts. I am forever indebted to them.

## Inquiries About Quilts

Should you be interested in purchasing quilts shown in this book please send a self-addressed, stamped envelope for a listing of available quilts and their prices to:

Nancy Crow
10545 Snyder Church Road
Baltimore, Ohio 43105
(614)862-6554

## Sources

The Nancy Crow line of quiltmaking products: Quickline I; Quickline II, 12", 18", 24"; Quick Templates; and the Quick Erase Marking Pencils are distributed by:
E-Z International
130 Grand Street
Carl-Stadt, New Jersey 07072
1-(201)935-9005

(E-Z International is the distributor for the "Quickline" tools. Please contact them for the names of shops retailing the tools.)

## Workshop Information

QUILT/SURFACE
DESIGN SYMPOSIUM
(send for brochure)
Nancy Crow/Sister Linda Fowler
10545 Snyder Church Road
Baltimore, Ohio 43105
(614) 862-6554

(QUILT/SURFACE DESIGN SYM-POSIUM is a two-week symposium structured to offer serious quiltmakers a range of classes that include: Painting on Fabric, Techniques of Texture, Design, Machine Applique, Dyeing Fabrics, Surface Techniques, Independent Study, Commission Work. The emphasis will be on "quiltmaking as an art form." This will be an annual symposium.)

# BIOGRAPHY

## Resume
Occupation: Artist
Medium: Contemporary Quiltmaking
Born: Loudonville, Ohio, 1943
Current Address: 10545 Snyder Church Road
Baltimore, Ohio 43105
(614)862-6554

## Education
| | | | |
|---|---|---|---|
| Ohio State University | BFA | 1965 | (Ceramics)(Textiles) |
| Ohio State University | MFA | 1969 | (Ceramics)(Textiles) |
| Mexico City College | Winter 1963 | | (Studied Art) |
| Columbus Cultural Arts Center | 1968-1969 | | (Studied Weaving) |
| Penland School of Crafts | Summer 1969 | | (Studied Weaving) |
| Arrowmont School of Arts/Crafts Summer 1972 | | | (Studied Weaving) |

## Awards
1988    *Award For Excellence*, Ohio Designer Craftsmen, "The Best of 1988"

1987    *Award For Excellence*, Ohio Designer Craftsmen, "The Best of 1987"

1986    Recipient of the Ohio Designer Craftsmen *Award For Outstanding Achievement:* It states that Nancy Crow has been recognized by fellow colleagues and professional as having made a major contribution to crafts in Ohio through creative and technical excellence, the broadening of the field of knowledge and in professional accomplishments that will be an enduring inspiration for future generations.

## Grants
1988    *Individual Artist's Fellowship For $10,000.00,* The Ohio Arts Council.

1985    *Individual Artist's Fellowship,* The Ohio Arts Council.

1982    *Individual Artist's Fellowship,* The Ohio Arts Council.

1980    *Craftsman's Fellowship,* The National Endowment for the Arts.

1980    *Individual Artist's Fellowship,* The Ohio Arts Council.

## Poster
1986    In celebration of its 30th year, The American Craft Museum in New York City, published a poster using my quilt, BITTERSWEET XIV.

## Quilt National
In 1978 I thought up the idea of organizing a professional juried exhibition that would promote contemporary quilts. This project was undertaken by a large group of volunteers and a year later in July 1979, the first Quilt National opened in Athens, Ohio. This exhibition was so successful and so well-attended that it has since become a biennial event and international in scope. It is one of the highest quality exhibitions of contemporary quilts held in the United States.

## Collections
1987    The Ohio Governor's Mansion. My quilt, CONTRADICTIONS, was chosen as the first purchase by the Ohio Arts Council for the Governor's Residence Art Collection.

1987    Mark Levine, New York City.

1986    Christina Bigler, Switzerland, (C.B.B. Imports/Exports)
The Vantage Companies, Atlanta, Georgia

1985    Jack Lenor Larsen, New York City.

1984    The American Craft Museum, New York City.
Ohio Bell Telephone Company
Ashland Chemical Company

1983    General Foods Corporate Headquarters
Southwest General Hospital

1981    Museum of American Folk Art, New York City
Islamabad Consulate, Washington, D.C.

1980    The Massillon Museum of Art, Massillon, Ohio.

1979    K–Mart International World Headquarters

## Books and Magazines (in which my quilts have appeared)
1987    4-page color spread on my quilts in *Japan Quilts*.

1986    *Craft Today: Poetry of the Physical*, Paul J. Smith and Edward Lucie-Smith, American Craft Museum.
*The Art Quilt*, Penny McMorris and Michael Kile, *Quilt Digest.*
*The Complete Book of Quiltmaking*, Michele Walker, Alfred A. Knopf, New York.

1985    *The State of the Art Quilt*, Barbara Packer, Editor, Quilt Expo 85.
*Quilts: The State of an Art,* Quilt National '85 Catalogue.

1984    *The Contemporary Quilt*, Pattie Chase, Catalogue for quilt exhibit touring Japan in 1984 and 1985.

1983    *Design Through Discovery*, ( My quilt used for cover of book.), Holt, Rinehart & Winston, New York.
*American Crafts: A Sourcebook for the Home*, Katharine Pearson, Stewart, Tabori and Chang, New York.
*American Decorative Arts*, Robert Bishop and Patricia Coblentz, Harry N. Abrams, Inc., New York.
*The Quilts: New Directions for an American Tradition*, Quilt National '83 catalogue.
"Decorative Design," quarterly published by Gakkenary Books, Tokyo, Japan, December 1983.
*A Loving Study of American Patchwork Quilts*, Kei Kobayashi, Bunka Publishing Bureau, Tokyo, Japan.
*Textilforum*, German Textile Magazine.
"Architectural Digest," Knapp Communications Corp., Los Angeles, California. (My quilt: BITTERSWEET XII appeared in July issue.)
"PD Magazine," *St. Louis Post Dispatch*, St. Louis, Missouri.

1982    *The Quiltmaker's Art,* Fiberarts Magazine, Asheville, North Carolina (My quilt BITTERSWEET XIV featured on cover)
*Contemporary Quilting*, Sharon Robinson, Davis Publications.
*A Life Planning Guide For Women*, Mary Vendor Goot, Paideia Press, My quilt NOVEMBER STUDY I, appears on the cover.
Quilt Engagements Calendar, Cyril I. Nelson, E.P. Dutton & Co., New York.
*Quilting I and Quilting II*, Penny McMorris, Two books produced in conjunction with the television series produced for National Educational Broadcasting by Bowling Green State University, WBGU-TV, Bowling Green, Ohio.

1981    *Crib Quilts and Other Small Wonders,* Thos. K. Woodard & Blanche Greenstein, E.P. Dutton & Co.
*The Fiberarts Design Book*, Fiberarts Magazine, Asheville, North Carolina.
*The New American Quilt,* Quilt National '81 catalogue.
*The Quilt Engagement Calendar*, Cyril I. Nelson, E.P. Dutton Co.
*The Second Quiltmaker's Handbook*, Michael James, Prentice-Hall.

1978    *The Quiltmaker's Handbook*, Michael James, Prentice-Hall.
*The Wool Quilt*, Jean Dubois, LaPlata Press.

## Exhibitions
1989    "Governor's Residence Art Collection," Governor's Mansion, Columbus, Ohio, Oct. 6, 1988-August 31, 1989.
Invitational, "Ohio Perspectives: New Work In Metal, Textiles, and Clay," The Akron Art Museum, Akron, Ohio, Nov. 5-Jan. 15, 1989.
Invitational, "The Works Gallery," Philadelphia, PA, March-May.
Invitational, "Dawson Gallery," Albany, New York, June 30-Aug. 8.
Invitational, "Worthington Arts Council:" August 1989.
"One Woman Exhibition," Quilts Unlimited, Williamsburg, VA, Oct. 1989
"Design In America," the work of 24 artists was chosen to tour Eastern European countries, sponsored by the United States Information Agency, Washington, D.C. (from 1986-1990)

1988    "Ohio Perspectives: New York In Metal, Textiles and Clay," The Akron Art Museum, Akron, Ohio, Nov. 5-Jan 15, 1989.
"Invitational," The Zanesville Art center, Zanesville, Ohio, Nov. 6-26, 1988.
"Invitational, 1988 Pacesetter," The Ohio Designer Craftsmen Gallery, Columbus, Ohio, Oct. 18-Nov. 24, 1988.
"Invitational, Contemporary Quilt/Furniture Show," Kerns Art Center, Eugene, Oregon, Oct. 7-Nov. 27, 1988.
Eve Mannes Gallery, Atlanta, Georgia, July 1988.
"Invitational," Vermont State Craft Center, Middlebury, Vermont, June 11-July 14, 1988.
"The Artist As Quiltmaker III," Fava Gallery, Oberlin, Ohio, May 29-July 24, 1988.

Invitational, "Quilts Not To Sleep With," The Wilson Arts Center, Rochester, New York, April 8-May 6, 1988.

Invitational, "We The Women," Metropolitan Museum and Art Center, Coral Gables, Florida, March 6-27, 1988.

Invitational, "Quilts and Coverups," Louisville Art Gallery, Louisville, Kentucky, Jan. 18-Feb. 26, 1988.

Invitational, "Advancing Tradition," Sandusky Cultural Center, Sandusky, Ohio, Jan. 10-31, 1988.

1987 My quilt included in the exhibit, "Poetry Of The Physical," was shown at The Denver Art Museum, Laguna Art Museum, Phoenix Art Museum.

"Poetry Of The Physical," the "Inaugural Exhibition" of the new American Craft Museum, New York, New York, Sept. 30, 1986-Feb. 1987. (This show travels for two years across U.S.)

"The Art Quilt," Los Angeles Municipal Art Museum, Los Angeles, California, Sept. 30-Nov. 14, 1986 & then travels for two years across the U.S.

"Design In America," Official Invitational (24 artists chosen & my quilt the only quilts) Exhibition to tour Eastern Europe & sponsored by the United States Information Agency, 1986-1989.

"Two Women Exhibition, Nancy Crow/Martha Crow," Curfman Gallery, Colorado State University, Ft. Collins, Colorado, Nov. 9-Dec. 11.

Invitational, The New England Quilt Museum, Lowell, Massachusetts.

Invitational, The Hand and the Spirit Gallery, Scottsdale, Arizona.

Invitational, "Show of Shows," Southeastern Ohio Cultural Arts Center, June 8-July 10, Athens, Ohio.

Invitational, Mansfield Arts Center, Mansfield, Ohio, July 19-Aug. 23.

Invitational, Pennsylvania State University Museum of Art, June 28-Aug. 30.

Invitational, Arkansas Decorative Art Museum, Little Rock, Arkansas, May 15-July 22.

"The 77th Annual Columbus Art League Exhibition," Columbus Museum of Art, May 30-July 26.

"Poetry Of The Physical," The "Inaugural Exhibition" of the new American Craft Museum, New York, New York, Sept. 30, 1986-Feb. 1987. (Then it travels for two years across U.S.)

"The Art Quilt," Los Angeles Municipal Art Museum, Los Angeles, California, Sept.30-Nov.14, 1986 & then travels for three years across the U.S.

"Design In America," Official Invitational 24 artists chosen & my quilts the only quilts) Exhibition to tour Eastern Europe & sponsored by the United States Information Agency, Washington, D.C. 1986-1989.

Invitational, Santa Monica Heritage Museum, Santa Monica, California, July 1987.

1986 "Two Women Exhibition, Nancy Crow: Quilts and Martha Crow: Paintings," Spangler-Cummings Gallery, Columbus, Ohio, Oct. 3-Nov. 28, 1986.

"Fiber 15," Invitational, "Materials Images:15 Fiber Artists," School of Art Gallery, Bowling Green State University, Bowling Green, Ohio, Aug. 25-Sept. 16, 1986.

"Quilt Magic," Rochester Museum & Science Center, Rochester, New York, Sept. 12-28, 1986.

"All Ohio 1986," The Canton Art Institute, Canton, Ohio, Sept. 13-Oct. 31, 1986.

"First Annual Governor's Residence Art collection," I was one of 37 Ohio artists chosen to have a work included in this year long exhibition, Governor's Mansion, Columbus, Ohio, Sept. 1985-Sept. 1986. (Also chosen for 1987.)

"The Best of 1986," Columbus Cultural Arts Center, Columbus, Ohio, March 16-April 26, 1986.

"Color: The Spectrum of Expression," North Carolina State University, Raleigh, North Carolina, March 14-May 11, 1986.

"Eleventh Biennial National Invitational Crafts Exhibition," Illinois State University, Normal, Illinois, Feb. 25-March 23, 1986.

"Contemporary Quilts," Darmouth College, Hopkins Center, Hanover, New Hampshire, Jan. 17-March 7, 1986.

"Quilting: New Images From An Old Tradition," The Gallery at Hastings-On-Hudson, Hastings-On-Hudson, New York, Dec. 8-Jan. 19, 1986.

"American Baskets and Quilts: New Forms From Old Traditions," The Woodmere Art Museum, Philadelphia, Pennsylvania, Nov.

10-Jan. 5.

1985 "One Woman Exhibition of Quilts," Gallery 1550, Clarke College, Dubuque, Iowa, Sept. 1-31, 1985.

"1985 Ohio Selection," (my quilts were chosen to be included after studio visit by the curator), The Dayton Art Institute, Dayton, Ohio, Aug. 17-Sept. 29, 1985.

"'85 Quilt Market Fashion Show," Fairfield Processing Corporation, Danbury, Connecticut.

"Vermont Quilt Festival," Rutland, Vermont, July 11-14, 1985.

"Contemporary Decorative Functional Crafts," Stifel Fine Arts Center, Oglebay Institute, Wheeling, West Virginia, June 29-Aug. 31, 1985.

"Quilt National '85," The Dairy Barn, Athens, Ohio, June 7-July 7, 1985.

"Fabrications," Missoula Museum of the Arts, Missoula, Montana, Apr. 20-June 15, 1985.

"Quilt Expo '85," Sands Point Preserve, Hempstead House, Middleneck Road, Sands Point, New York, Apr. 18-28, 1985.

"Contemporary Quilts," Berea College Art Gallery, Berea, Kentucky, March 1-25, 1985.

"Fiber Invitational," Lynn Mayhew Gallery, Ohio Wesleyan University, Delaware, Ohio, Feb. 11-March 1, 1985.

1984 "One Woman Exhibition of Quilts, Tapestries, Ceramics," Ohio University Branch/Lancaster Gallery, Feb. 12-March 11.

"Invitational," North Carolina State University, School of Design Gallery, Raleigh, North Carolina, March 12-27.

"One Woman Exhibition of Quilts," Indianapolis Museum of Art, Indianapolis, Indiana, Apr. 3-29.

Invitational, "Quilts Contemporains Americans,"France (traveling show of American quilts July 1, 1984-1985).

Invitational, "Quilting: A Modern Tradition," Southeastern Massachusetts University, North Darmouth, Massachusetts, Oct. 9-3.

Invitational, "Contemporary American Quilts in Japan," (touring Japan from Sept. 6, 1984-March 1985).

1983 "One Woman Exhibition of Quilts," Objects Gallery,San Antonio, Texas, Sept.-Oct. 1983.

"Pattern," American Craft Museum, New York City, Oct. 23, 1982-Jan. 31, 1983.

1982 Carol Hooberman Gallery, Birmingham, Michigan, November 1-31.

Craftsman Gallery, "Folk Art Influence In Contemporary American Crafts," Scarsdale, New York, July 15-Aug. 21.

"Ulster County Quilt Exposition '82," New York State, June 12-20.

One Woman Exhibition, "The Thread Connection," June 12-July 17.

"59th Annual Spring Show," Erie Art Center, Erie, Pennsylvania, Apr. 24-June 13.

May Show, Cleveland Museum of Art, Cleveland, Ohio, Apr. 21-May 30.

One Woman Exhibition, Lima Art Association, Lima, Ohio, March 7-31.

Invitational, Schumacher Gallery, Capital University, Columbus, Ohio, March 7-28.

"Fiber: Cloth Forms," Dayton Art Institute, Dayton, Ohio, March 3-June 5.

Invitational, Rockwell Gallery, Boston, Massachusetts, Feb. 15-May 30.

"New Directions: Clay and Fiber," East Carolina University, Greenville, North Carolina, Feb. 18-March 21.

"Ohio Quilts: A Living Tradition," Canton Art Institute, Canton, Ohio, Jan. 28-March 15.

Invitational, "American Tradition: Contemporary Interpretation," Sign of the Swan, Philadelphia, Pennsylvania, Jan. 21-Feb. 20.

Invitational, First St. Forum, St. Louis, Missouri, Jan. 15-March 15.

1981 Invitational, "Contemporary Quilts," Colburn Gallery, Kenyon College, Gambier, Ohio, Jan. 15-Feb. 8, 1981.

Invitational, "6 Ohio Artists/6 Indiana Artists," Cranbrook Academy of Art Museum, Bloomfield Hills, Michigan, Jan. 25-March 1, 1981.

Invitational, "Contemporary Quilting: A Renaissance," University of Wisconsin-Green Bay, Green Bay, Wisconsin, Feb. 1 1981-Aug. 31, 1982.

Invitational, "Contemporary Quilts," Millersville State College, Millersville, Pennsylvania, Feb. 18-March 14, 1981.

"Sixth Invitational Fibers Exhibition," Springfield Art Association, Springfield, Illinois, March 7-Apr. 25, 1981.

Invitational, "Contemporary Appalachian Quilt Exhibition," Southern Alleghenies Museum of Art, Loretto, Pennsylvania, March 28-May 3, 1981.

Invitational, "A Patchwork Garden," The Hunter Museum of Art, Chattanooga, Tennessee, Apr.-May 3, 1981.

Invitational, Valentine Museum, Richmond, Virginia, Apr. 1-30.

Invitational, "Ohio Quilt," The College of Wooster Frick Art Museum, Wooster, Ohio, Apr. 5-May 3, 1981.

"One Woman Show," St. Louis, Missouri, Apr. 5-May 15, 1981.

"1981 May Show," The Cleveland Museum of Art, Cleveland, Ohio, May 6-June 7, 1981.

"jubilee 50," The League of New Hampshire Craftsmen, Currie Gallery of Art, Manchester, New Hampshire, June 20-Sept. 7, 1981.

Invitational, "History of American Quilts," The Museum of the Southwest, Midland, Texas, Aug. 8-Oct. 18, 1981.

Invitational, "Two Women Exhibition of Quilts," S.O.M.A.C.E., Portsmouth, Ohio, Aug. 23-Oct. 4, 1981.

Invitational, Phebe Conley Gallery, California State University, Fresno, California, September 1-30, 1981.

"One Woman Exhibition of Quilts," Roanoke College, Salem, Virginia, Sept. 12-Oct. 18, 1981.

Invitational, "The Quilted Idiom," The Hand and the Spirit Crafts Gallery, Scottsdale, Arizona, Oct. 1-31, 1981.

"Quilt National '81," Athens, Ohio, July 2-26, 1981.

1980    "American Crafts," Springfield Art Association, Springfield, Illinois, Nov. 22, 1980-Jan. 3, 1981.

Invitational, America House, Tenafly, New Jersey, Oct. 18-Nov. 14, 1980.

"Three Women Exhibition" (Martha Crow – paintings; Mary Crow – poetry; Nancy Crow – quilts), The Mather Gallery, Case Western Reserve University, Cleveland, Ohio, Oct. 12-Nov. 3.

Ohio State Fair, Professional Fine Arts Exhibit, "Second Best of Show Award," Columbus, Ohio, Aug. 11-24, 1980.

"Quilt Invitational," Artlink Artspace, Fort Wayne, Indiana, June 14-July 22, 1980.

"Quilt Invitational," Ulster County Quilt Exposition 1980, Stone Ridge, New York, June 13-17, 1980.

Quilt Invitational, "Appalachiana," Bethesda, Maryland, May 18-June 8, 1980.

Invitational, "Art For Use," American Craft Museum, New York City, Apr. 15-May 25, 1980.

"The May Show," The Cleveland Museum of Art, received the "Horace E. Potter Memorial Award For excellence In Craftsmanship," Cleveland, Ohio, Apr. 16-May 18, 1980.

"One Woman Exhibition of Quilts," The Massillon Museum of Art, Massillon, Ohio, March 1980.

Invitational, Pajaro Valley Quilt Association, Aptos, California, Feb. 1980.

Invitational, American Craft Museum organized for Winter Olympics, Center For Music, Drama and Art, Fine Art Gallery, Lake Placid, New York, February 2-29, 1980.

Invitational, Kilcawley Center Art Gallery of Youngstown State University, Youngstown, Ohio, Jan. 23-Feb. 8, 1980.

Invitational, Contemporary Quilt Exhibit, Le Moyne Art Foundation, Tallahassee, Florida, Jan. 11-Feb. 10, 1980.

"Two Women Exhibition," Arizona State University, Memorial Union Gallery, Tempe, Arizona, Jan.-Feb. 1980.

1979    Three Women Exhibition, "Contemporary Quilts," Baldwin-Wallace College, Berea, Ohio, Nov. 4-Dec. 2, 1979.

"International Quilt Invitational," Stedelijk Museum, Schiedam, Holland, Oct. 1979.

"Beaux Arts Designer/Craftsmen '79," Columbus Museum of Art, Columbus, Ohio, Sept. 16-Nov. 4, 1979.

Ohio State Fair, Professional Fine Arts Exhibit, "Best of Show Award," Columbus, Ohio.

"Two Women Exhibition of Quilts," The Mansfield Art Center, Mansfield, Ohio, Sept. 1979.

"Quilt National '79," Athens, Ohio, June 15-July 8, 1979.

"Quilt Invitational," Michigan State University, East Lansing, Michigan, May 1979.

"The May Show," The Cleveland Museum of Art, "Juror's Mention For Quilt," Apr. 11-May 13, 1979.

"Midwest Surface Design '79," Kent State University, Kent, Ohio, March 26-Apr. 15, 1979.

"Quilt Invitational," Hunter Museum of Art, Chattanooga, Tennessee, Apr. 1-22, 1979.

1978    "Ohio Designer/Craftsman Traveling Show," One Quilt, Columbus, Ohio.

"One Woman Exhibition of Quilts," Indiana-Purdue University, Aug. 1978.

"The May Show," The Cleveland Museum of Art, Cleveland, Ohio.

"The May Show," Mansfield Art Center, "Juror's Award For Quilt."

1977    "One Woman Exhibition of Quilts," Seigfred Gallery, Ohio University, Athens, Sept. 1977.

"The May Show," The Cleveland Museum of Art, "Juror's Mention For Quilt."

"May Show Invitational," Gallery 200, Columbus, Ohio.

Invitational, Columbus Gallery of Fine Arts, Columbus, Ohio.

"Liturgical Art VI," Capital University, Feb. 1977.

1976    "Quilt Invitational," Huntington Gallery, Columbus, Ohio, Oct. 1976.

"Ohio Artists and Craftsmen Invitational," Massillon Museum of Fine Arts, Massillon, Ohio, Oct. 1976.

"Ohio Patchwork '76," Fine Arts Gallery, Bowling Green State University, Aug. 1976.

"Quilts, Four Women Invitational," Columbus Gallery of Fine Arts, Columbus, Ohio, May 1976.

Invitational, Gallery 200, Columbus, Ohio, May 1976.

"Quilt Invitational," Mansfield Art Center, Mansfield, Ohio, Jan. 1976.

"Five Ohio Artists/Craftsmen Invitational, " Studio San Guiseppe, College of Mt. St. Joseph, Ohio, Jan. 1976.

❖ *(Left:) My biography could not be complete without mentioning a most important part of my life, my sons, Nathaniel John Stitzlein (left) and Matthew Crow Stitzlein (right). 1988.*